Good Fortune

My Journey to Gold Mountain

To my late husband, Roger L. Wong,
who spent countless hours on the computer
typing the manuscript for me.

And to Kirby Wong, Karen Weller,
Amanda Wong, Brian Weller, and Andrea Weller.

Without the support and encouragement
of my family and friends,
I would never have been able to write this book.
You know who you are.

Good Fortune

My Journey to Gold Mountain

Li Keng Wong

PEACHTREE
ATLANTA

Ω
Published by
PEACHTREE PUBLISHERS
1700 Chattahoochee Avenue
Atlanta, Georgia 30318-2112

www.peachtree-online.com

Book design by Loraine M. Joyner and Melanie McMahon Ives

Printed in the United States of America
10 9 8 7 6 5 4 3 2 1
First Edition

The Chinese characters on the front of the book reading from top to bottom represent Spirit, Courage, Happiness, and Destiny.

Library of Congress Cataloging-in-Publication Data

Wong, Li Keng.
 Good fortune / by Li Keng Wong.-- 1st ed.
    p. cm.
 Includes bibliographical references and index.
    ISBN 1-56145-367-6 (alk. paper)
1. Wong, Li Keng--Juvenile literature. 2. Chinese Americans--California--Oakland--Biography--Juvenile literature. 3. Immigrants--California--Oakland--Biography--Juvenile literature. 4. Chinatown (Oakland, Calif.)--Biography--Juvenile literature. 5. Oakland (Calif.)--Biography--Juvenile literature. 6. Chinese Americans--California--Oakland--History--20th century--Juvenile literature. 7. United States--Emigration and immigration--History--20th century--Juvenile literature. 8. China--Emigration and immigration--History--20th century--Juvenile literature. I. Title.
 F869.O2W65 2006
 979.4'66004951--dc22
                                        2005027856

Table of Contents

1—A Letter from Gold Mountain 1

2—Waiting 5

3—Joyful Times 7

4—Mama's Story 11

5—The Coaching Papers 15

6—A Gold Mountain Guest 19

7—On Our Way 25

8—A Strange New World 29

9—Aboard the SS Hoover 35

10—Crossing the Pacific 39

11—Locked Up 43

12—A Sweet Surprise 47

13—Yee's Interrogation 49

14—Questions for Li Hong 51

15—My Turn 53

16—Good-bye to Angel Island 55

17—Ferry to Freedom 59

18—Welcome to Chinatown 63

19—A Small Celebration 67

20—Exploring Our New Home 69

21—Back to School 71

22—Homecoming 75

23—A New Beginning 77

24—Playing the Lottery 81

25—A New Member of the Family 85
26—A Red Egg Party 87
27—Troubles 91
28—Another Chance..93
29—Life in Chinatown...95
30—Ghosts 99
31—Changes 105
32—Helping the Family..109
33—Dark Days...113
34—A New Life...117
35—Good Luck at Last...121
36—A Very Special Year......................................125
Author's Note...129
More about Angel Island Immigration Station
and the Chinese Exclusion Act...............................133
For Further Information......................................136
About the Author...137

Chapter 1

A Letter from Gold Mountain

Mama, when will Baba come home?" I asked.

"Don't be so impatient, Li Keng," Mama replied. "Your father's letter just arrived. I'll find out as soon as I read it."

"But we don't even have a picture of Baba," I complained. "It has been so long since we've seen him that I hardly remember him. All I know is that he works in Gum Saan."

Gum Saan means "Gold Mountain" in Chinese. It also means the United States. To all of us children in our rural village in China, Gold Mountain seemed like a magical place that was very, very far away.

"All the other families in our village have a father at home," I went on. "But we don't, and I don't like it."

My mother sighed. Of the three girls in our family, I was the whiner. I always pestered my mother with many questions. Sometimes she smiled, but sometimes she glared at me when my questions annoyed her. Mama was very strict. She often scolded me for talking too much.

My name is Gee Li Keng. Gee is our family name. Chinese people always put their last names first. Li means "beautiful" and Keng means "jade." In April 1933 I turned seven years old. It was around that time that we received the letter from Baba.

We lived in a rural village called Goon Do Hung, which means "A Village of Good People." Life was slow paced and peaceful. Villagers trudged out to the fields each day to attend to their rice crops and small vegetable gardens. Water buffalo pulled plows to turn the soil. Everyone worked hard to survive.

Li Hong, my older sister, was eleven years old. She was the daughter from Baba's first wife, who died when Li Hong was a baby. Mama was Baba's second wife. Lai Wah, my younger sister, and I were Mama's daughters. Lai Wah was not quite three.

Our family had a maidservant named Fung, a teenager who helped Mama around the house. She bathed us, cooked all our meals, cleaned for us and, most importantly, she played with us. Mama brought her from a family in a nearby village. Baba had sent money from Gum Saan to do this. Mama explained to us girls, "Fung's family is very poor. They felt it was necessary for them to sell her to us so that they would have one less mouth to feed. Her family was almost starving."

Mama welcomed Fung as an oldest daughter. She relied on her for help and treated her kindly. We three girls enjoyed her company and loved her very much. But since there was no man in our house, I envied my playmates who had fathers at home.

"So why can't our Baba live with us?" I asked Mama now.

"Hush, Li Keng, you talk too much," Mama said. She sounded angry and frowned at me. "Your Baba works hard in Gold Mountain so that he can send money home to us. The money takes care of all our living expenses. We don't have to grow two rice crops each year like our neighbors. We buy our rice and vegetables. Our neighbors toil in the fields day in and day out from one year to the next just to put food on the table. We may not be rich, but we're better off than others."

I looked at the ground. I knew Mama was right.

"I know Baba is like a stranger to all of us," Mama continued. "And I know you want him at home. But there is nothing I can do to change this. Now I want you to go and find Li Hong and Lai Wah. I have good news to tell you girls."

Good news? Dashing outside, I grinned as I yelled to my sisters, "Li Hong! Lai Wah! Mama wants you two in the house right now. She has news for us. *Fai dee! Fai dee!* Hurry! Hurry!" I bossed them as if I were Mama.

The three of us rushed into our small kitchen. A letter written in Chinese was spread out on the table.

"Mama, we're back. Please tell us the good news," I begged.

"Girls, I received a letter from your Baba. He says he will be home in the ninth month, which is five months away."

"What day of the ninth month?" I interrupted Mama. In my excitement, I forgot good manners.

"Let me finish, Li Keng, and don't interrupt me again," Mama scolded. "Keep quiet now. Your Baba will arrive toward the end of the ninth month. He said he will take us back to Gold Mountain with him."

We girls smiled and clapped our hands in unison. Wow! Going to Gold Mountain? We could not believe what Mama had told us. We had no idea where Gold Mountain was, exactly, but we knew that this was indeed very good news.

Then I began to think. My mind tried to conjure up a picture of Baba. Did I look like him? And what would it be like to have a man in the house? What was Baba like as a person? Was he a gentle, kind, soft-spoken man like our next-door neighbor Hong, who always smiled and patted me on my head? Sometimes Hong gave my sisters and me rock candy as treats. We all liked him, but especially me. He always gave me the largest piece.

Or was Baba like another of our neighbors, Ping? He was a mean, nasty neighbor who screamed at his children and his wife. Sometimes he beat his children. I often heard his wife crying because of her misery and I covered my ears with my hands. Were other men as cruel as Ping?

How would Baba treat us? Mama said that the last time Baba came home from Gold Mountain was several years ago. I was too young to remember him. It would be wonderful if he was like Hong, our kind neighbor. But what if he was like Ping, who always gave me dark, angry looks and never smiled at me?

We would find out soon.

Chapter 2

WAITING

After Baba's letter arrived, I noticed that Mama was smiling more. Her steps seemed lighter, as though she were floating on air. She seemed happier because Baba was coming home again.

Every day I pestered Mama. "Did a letter come from Baba today? I'm tired of waiting!"

Mama frowned and answered, "Li Keng, that's enough. You're always so impatient. Whining isn't going to bring Baba's letter to us any faster. You're getting on my nerves. Stop it right now before I get a headache!"

"Yes, Mama," I answered, clamping my lips together. Then I raced outside so she wouldn't see that I was upset.

Li Hong stood and listened as Mama scolded me. My mouth always made trouble for me. But Li Hong was gentle and sweet. She never bugged Mama. She followed me out of the house as we headed toward the village square to play with the other children.

On the way we saw Cousin Soe. Cousin Soe was a widow and she had no children. She loved to play with us. "Come join us!" she called, waving.

Mama leased our land to Cousin Soe. Fung helped Cousin

Soe raise vegetables like cabbage, green onions, and bok choy, which is like Swiss chard. Every family but ours planted two rice crops a year. Most of the children in our village would have to plant rice in the paddies or weed the vegetable gardens when they grew older. But for now, young children could still play instead of working all day.

The boys and the girls of our village didn't play together. The girls played with the girls and the boys played with the boys. Sometimes the older boys showed off by treading water in the shallow lake with big, silly smiles on their faces. The girls usually ignored their antics. They turned their heads away.

Mama came out to check on us. "Your Li Hong is such a good girl," Cousin Soe said. "Could she sleep at my house at night to keep me company? I've been a widow for a year now and I am so lonely. She could go home in the mornings."

"What do you think, Li Hong? Do you want to do that?" Mama asked my sister.

Li Hong smiled and nodded yes.

I didn't say anything. I was sure I would miss my family too much to sleep at someone else's house, even Cousin Soe's. But Li Hong seemed happy.

That night I couldn't sleep. I missed Li Hong. But mostly I was still worried about the letter. I wanted to know exactly what Baba had planned for us.

Chapter 3

Joyful Times

Chinese people love all kinds of festivals. In Goon Do Hung we celebrated the New Year Festival, the Dragon Boat Festival, the Mid-Autumn Festival, and the Clear Brightness Festival. Festivals brought people together for fun and relaxation.

Everyone in our village looked forward to celebrating the Clear Brightness Festival, which was held in early April. This festival was held to honor each family's departed ancestors. The Chinese call this festival Ching Ming. Some families visit their ancestors' gravesites during this time. They bring food like rice, stir-fried vegetables, chicken, and sweet pastries. Before placing the food in front of the headstones, they tidy up the gravesites. They burn incense and bow three times to show respect to their ancestors.

Later, they picnic and play. Flying kites was a favorite pastime in our village.

Weeks before the festival that year in 1933, many families began making kites in all kinds of shapes, colors, and designs. Imaginations ran wild. Every kite was like a piece of art.

To take my mind off of worrying about Baba's letter, I went next door to Hong's house and offered to help his family make their kite. They had already started the design.

"May I help you?" I asked. "My family isn't making a kite this year. I can cut the shape, glue, and cut the string. Please?"

"Yes, Li Keng," Hong answered. His son and daughter seemed pleased also. I smiled.

On a table I saw colorful rice paper, bamboo sticks, strings, and a small dish of freshly cooked sticky rice. We typically ate sticky rice, but this sticky rice would be used to help glue the rice paper to the bamboo sticks.

We worked slowly and carefully. Hong cut out the shape of the kite as a big butterfly. We children concentrated as we carefully applied the glue.

Everyone smiled because the butterfly kite turned out beautifully. I felt good because I had helped. When I returned home I told my family about our big project.

We waited for a crisp, windy day in April to hold the Clear Brightness Festival. The celebration would last all day. Everyone in the village stopped work and joined in.

Mama smiled when she heard the loud jabbering of our neighbors.

"Let's join them!" I said eagerly.

"All right," Mama said. "We will visit our ancestors' gravesites another day. I want all of us to have fun today. This made us girls very happy.

Fung held on to Lai Wah's hand and carried our basket of food. Li Hong walked with me. We hurried to the grassy slope of a small hill where everyone had assembled. We sat on the grass and turned our eyes skyward.

A strong wind carried the colorful kites up, up, and away. It seemed as though the many kites almost blocked out the sun. There were kites that looked like creatures such as butterflies, frogs, crabs, centipedes, and bats. There were many other designs, too. The villagers smiled, clapped, and yelled, "*Ho! Ho!* Good! Good!"

"Mama, I helped to put together the yellow and orange butterfly kite," I said excitedly. "Can you see it way up there?"

"Yes, Li Keng, it's beautiful!" Mama replied.

We ate cookies and cakes and chewed watermelon seeds as we watched. Everyone stayed out until the sun slowly disappeared from the horizon. Then the villagers trudged home tired and happy. I wished Baba had been there to see my kite.

Chapter 4
Mama's Story

One night after the Clear Brightness Festival, Mama gathered us in the kitchen.

"Do you girls want to hear the story of how I married your Baba in the year 1925?" she asked.

"Yes, yes!" we three girls yelled. We had never heard this story.

"Well, your Baba had been living in Gold Mountain since 1912. He married for the first time in 1921." Mama smiled at Li Hong. "You were born in 1922. And as you know, your mama died when you were hardly more than a baby.

"Baba's mother, your old grandmother, couldn't take care of Li Hong," Mama went on. "She begged Baba to come home to marry again so that his new wife could be Li Hong's mama."

We all nodded.

"So Baba obeyed his mother," Mama said. "He made a trip home from Gold Mountain to Goon Do Hung in 1925."

"Mama, I'm your oldest child, then?" I asked.

"Yes, you are, Li Keng," Mama answered. "Let me continue the story. Your grandmother hired a lady marriage broker, or *Mooey Yen Paw* to help her. Her name was Fong Paw Paw. Chinese people call an older lady "Paw Paw." The marriage broker wrote down Baba's name in Chinese, Seow Hong Gee, and his date of birth.

"Grandmother urged Fong Paw Paw to work quickly because Baba needed to return to Gold Mountain as soon as possible to work.

"The marriage broker walked from one village to another. She came to my village, the Yee village. It wasn't very far from the Gee village.

"She spoke to my mother and asked her, 'Do you have a daughter of marriageable age?' Then she saw me standing right next to my mother. 'What is your daughter's name?' Fong Paw Paw asked. 'How old is she?'

"The marriage broker looked at me closely. I blushed because I felt shy.

"My mother replied, 'My daughter's name is Suey Ting Yee. She was born in 1907. She is eighteen years old now and she wants to get married.'

"I didn't say a word. I let my Mama do all the talking. It was true. I did want to marry.

"Fong Paw Paw said, 'I know a Gold Mountain man. His name is Seow Hong Gee. He is a good catch because he has a fine job and can support your daughter.'

"My mama said, 'Yes, Suey Ting may marry Seow Hong Gee. Their birth dates match well. Go back to Seow Hong Gee's village and tell him the answer is yes.'

"I smiled to let Mama know that it was fine with me, too. Chinese people had been arranging marriages for their sons and daughters all through history.

"The *Mooey Yen Paw* walked back to Goon Do Hung. 'I have found a good looking and strong young lady for your son,' she reported to your grandmother and your Baba.

"Baba and Grandmother checked the calendar for a lucky date for the marriage to take place.

"On the big day, my mother and lady cousins dressed me in a red silk embroidered jacket and a beautiful red silk skirt with side pleats. As you know, red means good luck in Chinese. I looked as if I were a fine noble lady.

"Mother hired two strong men and a sedan chair to carry me to Goon Do Hung. The wooden sedan chair, lacquered in bright red, added color to the special day. I sat behind a closed curtain. My mother sent a cousin to accompany me. My family wouldn't be able to attend the wedding.

"It wasn't long before we arrived. I heard excited voices saying, '*Sun nang lai la!* The bride is here!'

"The men gently set the sedan chair down on the ground. Baba kicked the sedan chair softly and pulled the curtain apart. He looked at me for the first time and nodded his head. There was a little smile on his face.

"I glanced at him quickly. Then I kept my eyes down because it would have been very rude to not do so. I thought Baba looked fine.

"The villagers clapped and smiled as I stepped out of the sedan chair. Baba escorted me to his house where his mother waited with a few close relatives. Your white-haired grandmother sat like a queen and motioned for Baba and me to come forward. My cousin poured tea into a cup with no handle. I picked up the teacup with both hands and kowtowed three times. Kowtow means to bow.

"Your grandmother smiled and accepted the tea. Then she placed a beautiful pair of bracelets on the tray for me as my wedding gift. Baba also kowtowed to Grandmother.

"The simple tea ceremony completed our marriage. We

became man and wife. Then Baba gave me two American gold coin bracelets as his wedding gift to me. I loved the bracelets.

"Friends came into the house and wished us long life and happiness. They drank tea and ate Chinese pastries. Everyone left before it got dark.

"I had to stay for three days with your Baba and your grandmother. Then my cousin escorted me back to the Yee village to see my mother and family and pay my respects. I dressed in my good clothes for the trip home.

"My lady cousin poured tea in a cup. I bowed before my mother and handed the teacup to her with both hands.

"My mother smiled and accepted the tea. Then she drank the tea and gave me a package of *lay see,* which is money wrapped in paper.

"I only stayed for an hour because I had to return to the Gee village to start a new life with your Baba and grandmother.

"Baba stayed home in Goon Do Hung for another month before he sailed back to Gold Mountain. Li Keng, you were born in 1926. Baba made another trip to Goon Do Hung in 1930. Lai Wah, you were born in 1931."

Li Hong and I were fascinated by Mama's story. Even Lai Wah was listening carefully.

"I really don't know your Baba well," Mama went on. "But he has always taken good care of us by sending money home. He is a good man. I'm excited and happy that he is coming home in the ninth month. I hope his letter will come soon."

We girls clapped our hands.

"Mama, thank you for telling us this great story," I said.

Now we were all looking forward even more to living with Baba in Gold Mountain.

Chapter 5
THE COACHING PAPERS

One day a packet of papers arrived for our family. The courier who delivered the packet had to walk to our house from the nearest town to our village because there was no mail service to the village.

Once again Mama gathered us girls in the kitchen. With trembling hands, she carefully slit open the packet. There was a letter inside along with several other pages filled with writing.

Mama was the only woman in the village who could read and write in Chinese.

Once I had asked her, "Mama, how come you're the only woman in our village who can do this?"

"Your Baba said I must learn to read and write so that when he sends letters home, I won't have to depend on someone else to read them for me," Mama said. "He hired a teacher to tutor me in Chinese for two years. Your Baba is a wise man."

Now Mama read the letter and the rest of the pages in the packet. "Girls, these are coaching papers," Mama explained.

"What are coaching papers?" I interrupted.

"Coaching papers will help us answer the questions that the officials in Gold Mountain may ask us. Here are a few of them:

1. What is your name?
2. How old are you?
3. What is the name of your village?
4. How many people live there?
5. Who are your neighbors?"

I thought those questions seemed easy enough. Then Mama went on, "And here are some more for you girls:

6. You came with a lady. Is she your mama or your aunt?
7. Is your mother here with you?"

Our mother or our aunt? I thought those questions were very strange.

"We all must answer the questions correctly," Mama continued. "Baba says we must study the answers carefully. We must memorize the contents of this package so we won't make any mistakes. If we can't answer the questions correctly, the Gold Mountain officials will deport us back to China."

I didn't understand that at all. Send us back? Why would they do that? I had thought going to Gold Mountain would be easy if we had Baba to take us. But I knew better than to ask Mama any more questions. She was studying the letter and frowning.

"So, girls, we start to work on these questions immediately after lunch," Mama said. "Go out and play and give me some time to go over them. Don't wander off too far, do you hear me?"

"Yes, Mama." The three of us nodded.

"Li Hong and Lai Wah, I'll remind you two not to go too

far," I told my sisters. I liked being bossy. I often took charge because Li Hong sometimes forgot to follow instructions and Lai Wah was too young.

Fung prepared a lunch of boiled white rice, cabbage, and steamed sausage. We hurriedly gobbled our food as Mama sat at the kitchen table and spread out the sheets of thin rice paper with Chinese words all over them.

"Baba says these coaching papers will help us enter Gum Saan," Mama said. "Gold Mountain has laws which make it hard for Chinese people to go there. One of those laws says a Chinese laborer can't bring his wife to the United States."

Oh no! I thought. Does that mean Mama can't go to Gum Saan?

Mama took a deep breath. "I can't enter the United States as Baba's wife, but I can enter as his sister," she said. "Baba says we must lie about me, even though lying is bad. That is the only way for me to enter the United States with you girls."

Li Hong and Lai Wah's faces looked sad. I frowned. Mama had always taught us to tell the truth, but I guessed it was all right to lie in this case.

Mama continued, "Baba says you three girls must call me 'Yee' and not 'Mama.' 'Yee' means aunt in Chinese. You must not forget. If you call me 'Mama' in front of the officials, we will all be deported back to our village here in China. We'll be embarrassed because our neighbors will pity us. We'll never hear the end of it. So starting right now you must call me 'Yee.' Do you understand?"

My sisters and I nodded. Our mama would be our aunt from now on.

Chapter 6

A GOLD MOUNTAIN GUEST

We waited and waited for Baba to come home. Five months was a very long time.

Mama sent Li Hong and me to school. Lai Wah was too young to go.

"Your Baba wants you girls to be educated," Mama said. "You will go to the school in the next village until we leave. It is for both boys and girls. Fung will walk you there in the morning and she'll go back to wait for you after the end of classes. I want to make sure that you are safe."

In school, Li Hong and I learned calligraphy, which was writing Chinese characters with fine brushes. We memorized and practiced all the lessons taught to us.

My sister and I both did well in calligraphy. The teacher praised our efforts. "Your characters are like artwork," she said. "Keep practicing!"

I loved school and had no problems with my schoolwork. Li Hong, however, made many mistakes. The teacher often scolded her, "You didn't study hard enough. Hold out your left hand!" Then the teacher whacked Li Hong's palm once with a bamboo stick.

I cringed when I heard the sound. Poor Li Hong!

But Li Hong didn't cry. She just pulled her hand back, looking ashamed.

I gave the teacher an angry look. This teacher was really mean.

Li Hong and I didn't tell Mama what happened. Mama might be angry at Li Hong, too, for shaming our family.

Mama was very busy arranging a marriage for Fung. Fung had begged, "Please take me with you to Gum Saan. I promise to devote my life to taking care of your family. I don't want to marry now." Tears glistened in her eyes and she lowered her head.

Mama gently lifted Fung's chin. "I'm sorry, but we can't do that," she said gently. "We don't have the proper papers for you to emigrate with us. But I will try very hard to find you a good husband. We love you as a member of the family and we thank you for serving us so faithfully."

Mama kept her promise. She succeeded in locating a fine young man from a nearby village for Fung. Mama gave her gifts and some money to start a new life. When Fung left, we three girls lost a good friend. I missed her and felt sad. Li Hong and I also had to do more chores after Fung left.

In early summer, Paw Paw, Mama's mother, came to visit us. She would stay with us until we left for Gum Saan. "Hooray!" we girls yelled when Paw Paw arrived. All three of us loved our grandma, and she loved us back. She was a very sweet lady. Because of Paw Paw, I always loved and respected elderly people.

At last the ninth month arrived. On the twentieth day, Paw Paw, Mama, Li Hong, Lai Wah, and I waited nervously under the cool shade of an old oak tree. The old oak was a favorite public gathering spot for our village.

Finally we saw a sedan chair carried by wooden poles on the shoulders of two strong men. The chair was slowly lowered to the ground.

A few curious villagers quickly gathered to watch this unusual sight. Our village rarely had outside visitors. Everyone knew that someone of importance had arrived. How exciting! They spoke among themselves and smiled at us. "Gold Mountain Guest, a guest of America, is home. Look at his fancy clothes. He sure looks rich. Our village is honored by his return. Suey Ting's family is lucky."

People like my Baba who emigrated to the United States were called "Gold Mountain Guests" because they were not allowed to become citizens of the United States. The United States passed a law in 1882 called "The Chinese Exclusion Act." Chinese people were not allowed to become citizens. This law kept many Chinese from coming to the United States.

We watched a man wearing a suit and tie step down from the sedan chair. He had a big smile on his face.

Baba's eyes crinkled when he saw us. "*Fon lai la! Fon lai la!* I'm home! I'm home!" He looked at Mama first. He smiled at her and Paw Paw. Then he looked at us. There was no hugging or kissing, but he stooped to pat our heads. At the same time, he was making a happy laughing sound like, "Heh, heh, heh."

We three girls stood quietly and said, "Baba." All of us smiled at our father.

I stared at this stranger. He was short, like most of the people in our village. His big, dark brown eyes sparkled and his round, pale face contrasted with the dark-skinned villagers. He looked well fed, unlike the wiry men of our village. His suit was made of fine material. I thought I looked a little bit like him. My big eyes and round face were almost the same as his.

Baba seemed like a good person. At home he ate and played with us. His laughter echoed loudly and we reacted with big smiles. He grinned whenever he caught my eyes. I was so happy because he was not mean like Ping, the neighbor that I hated.

We saw Baba during the day, but he slept at a cousin's home at night. He explained that our small bedroom was too crowded. Mama accepted this arrangement.

He hovered over Mama, Li Hong, and me as we went over the coaching papers. "Be sure you remember all of the answers. The officials will be questioning you about many details," Baba patiently explained to us over and over. Paw Paw listened quietly.

"But Baba, we can't speak English. How will we understand the white people?" I asked nervously.

"Don't worry, Li Keng. The officials will have a Chinese interpreter. He will translate what we say into English," Baba replied.

This explanation calmed me down, but more questions popped into my mind. How far away from our village was Gold Mountain? How big was it? How long would it take us to travel there? What were white people like? Would they welcome us? Or would the officials trick us and send us back to China?

By this time, everyone in our village knew that we were embarking on a long journey to Gum Saan. Neighbors gathered under the old oak tree to share what they knew. "Li Keng's family is so lucky. They are going to Gold Mountain. Good for them!"

My heart jumped when Baba announced to us in early November, "We will leave on our journey in two days. Go to each house and say good-bye to our neighbors before we leave. We won't need many clothes or any other possessions. When we get to Hong Kong, we'll buy what we need before the journey."

"Why must we buy new clothes, Baba?" I asked.

"Your outfits look like cotton pajamas that are worn by poor laborers," Baba said. "We have to make a good impression when we get to Gum Saan, so you must wear clothes like the Americans wear.

"We'll depart early in the morning before the sun comes up," Baba went on. "It will still be dark. Until we get to Som Bot City, we'll walk quietly."

I asked Baba, "Why do we have to be quiet?"

I couldn't help feeling scared about so many things. Was there danger awaiting us beyond our village? Would Paw Paw be able to accompany us part of the way? Would we miss everyone in our village?

Would we come back to China someday for a visit? Would we like living in Gold Mountain? Would we make it to Gold Mountain safely?

Baba replied, "Li Keng, you worry too much about the unknown. Things will work out. Think positively."

"I'll try, Baba," I said. "Thank you."

But I still felt scared about our upcoming journey and the new life we would find in Gold Mountain.

Chapter 7
On Our Way

On the night before we were to leave, Paw Paw said to us, "I want to walk with you as far as Som Bot City. It may be the last time for me to see you." Smiling sadly, she cradled Lai Wah in her arms.

"Oh, Paw Paw, we'll miss you, too. We'll tell Baba to write letters to you." I wrapped my arms around her neck as I spoke.

At last the day came for us to depart. It was still dark when Mama gently shook the three of us girls awake. Paw Paw quietly helped Lai Wah get dressed and then warmed a big pot of rice gruel to fortify us. Chinese people call this porridge *jook*. Everyone slurped quietly and finished quickly.

Four male neighbors were standing outside our front door. "Our kind neighbors will help escort us until we get to Som Bot City," Baba said. "It's not too far, only an hour's walk."

I noticed that the men were carrying crude shovels and large farming tools. "Why are they carrying those?" I asked.

Baba said, "Shhh, Li Keng. I want to make sure that we will be safe. Our country has bandits roaming the rural areas to rob and murder innocent people. There are no policemen to protect us out here in the country, though there are policemen in cities. We must be very quiet as we walk so that bandits will not be aware of us."

Li Hong, Lai Wah, and I looked at each other. We were scared. Bandits! I hoped no bandits were waiting for us.

Baba quickly closed our front door. The men helped carry two suitcases. We only took one change of clothing. Paw Paw carried Lai Wah on her back.

We walked for one hour until we arrived in Som Bot City. We were tired and hungry, but luckily we did not meet any bandits.

We left Paw Paw and our neighbors in Som Bot City. I noticed that my grandmother wiped the streaming tears from her face with the sleeve of her good jacket. Mama's face was also wet with tears. Paw Paw hugged Mama like a mother bear hugging her precious cub.

Baba gave some money to the four men. "This is a small token of appreciation for your help. Thank you very much. Paw Paw, you walk carefully back to your village. The four gentlemen will escort you home. You'll be safe. As soon as we arrive in Gum Saan, we'll write you. Good-bye."

We all waved good-bye to Paw Paw and our loyal neighbors. Paw Paw said to me, "I will love you always. Have a safe trip. I know you'll have a good life in Gum Saan."

Since Som Bot City was connected to Canton, our next destination, by water, Baba hired a small boat called a sampan. It was rowed with an oar from the stern. This sampan had a little covering formed by mats. We had never been on a sampan before.

The water gently flapped as the sampan moved. It soothed

Lai Wah and she fell asleep. I was too excited to sleep. Mama, Li Hong, and I looked at the countryside and took in the wonderful sights

About two hours later we arrived in Canton, a big city in southern China. We boarded a black train for Hong Kong. We had never been on a train either.

The scenery whizzed by as the train clicked along the track. We had never been on anything that moved so fast. "Look at the rice paddies!" I cried. "See that tall tower with writing on the wall!"

I never knew that China was so huge. All of us kept looking at the changing scenery as the train chugged along. I was amazed when vendors on the sides of the tracks loudly called out what they had for sale. "Li Hong! Lai Wah!" I said excitedly. "Look at the delicious rice plates. Look at the beef jerky. Look at the cookies. Wow!"

"You must be hungry. It's been several hours since we ate the *jook* at home. How about some rice plates for all of us? Do you want some beef jerky, too?"

Baba's questions brought big smiles to our faces.

"Thank you, Baba," we replied.

After eating, we three girls were tired and dozed off. Mama and Baba rested quietly, too. Everything was happening so fast. I couldn't believe that there were big cities like this. Would Gold Mountain have big cities, too?

Chapter 8
A Strange New World

We woke up as the train came to a screeching halt. Baba told us, "We have arrived at the next stop on our journey, the city of Hong Kong. The name means 'Fragrant Harbor.' It is very well known all over the world. Come along now, and watch your steps as you get off the train."

Mama and we girls did as we were told and followed Baba.

Baba hired four rickshaws. A rickshaw is a small two-wheeled passenger vehicle with a folding top, pulled by one man. People used them in the city like taxis. I had seen rickshaws before, but I had never ridden in one.

Baba gave instructions to the four men to take us to our hotel. Our rickshaws clicked-clacked along the streets as we headed for our destination.

Great mobs of people of different nationalities were everywhere, some hurrying and some walking. I had never seen so many people in my life. I felt crowded and I didn't like it.

Hong Kong was a city of bustling streets, with tall skyscrapers, stores of all description, vendors, restaurants, theaters, and people who all looked different from one another. Everything seemed to attract my attention. I had never seen such wondrous sights or heard such unusual sounds. The strange mixture of unfamiliar languages struck my ears. I wished I knew what the people were saying.

"Do you understand what they are saying, Baba?" I asked.

"No, I don't, Li Keng. I only understand Chinese and English," Baba replied.

I also observed strange-looking giants with beards and turbans on their heads, directing traffic. Whistles sounded as the giants waved their arms.

"Who are they, Baba?" I asked.

Mama, Li Hong, and Lai Wah just stared.

"They are Sikhs, from India. They wear turbans to cover their heads. They make good policemen because they are tall, strong, and good workers. They keep the traffic moving."

I had no idea what Baba was trying to tell us. How strange, I thought to myself.

The rickshaws finally stopped in front of our hotel in Hong Kong. To us it looked like a palace.

The hotel was on a clean, paved street jammed with people. After we entered I stared at the broad marble staircase, which led to an upper floor. Our rooms were on the second floor. But we didn't take the staircase. We stepped into something that seemed like a birdcage.

"Baba, what is this funny box we are in?" I asked. "Why don't we climb the stairs to go to our rooms?"

"This is an elevator, a machine that can go up and down. It is faster and easier for people who have many bags or can't walk well," Baba replied.

I shook my head. Another new thing for us to experience!

We rode up in the elevator. As soon as we settled in our

rooms, Baba said, "Rest up now. Then we'll go to the tailor shop on the street floor. Each of you will be measured and fitted with American-style clothes. We'll buy shoes, socks, blouses, skirts, sweaters, and wool coats for winter."

Winter clothes would be new for us also. Back in our village we never needed heavy clothes because the weather was usually warm.

After washing our faces and hands, my sisters and I rested on top of the beds. Soon Baba knocked on our door

"Are you ready to go downstairs to the tailor shop?" he asked.

"Yes, yes, Baba, we're ready now!" Li Hong, Lai Wah, and I answered in one voice. We were very excited.

We walked down the staircase this time and entered the tailor shop. A smiling Chinese gentleman bowed and gestured for us to enter.

"Welcome. Your Baba told me that you're going to Gum Saan and need new outfits. I'll make sure that you look like real Americans when you wear the finished garments. Let me measure you all, starting with the smallest young lady first."

Lai Wah smiled and her eyes sparkled. She enjoyed the attention of having the tailor measure her with a cloth tape. Then he measured Mama, Li Hong, and me.

"All your outfits will be ready by tomorrow," the tailor announced. "My people will work all night to get it done."

The tailor kept his promise. Early the next morning our garments were ready. They were beautiful and fit perfectly.

"I like my new clothes," I announced to everyone as my hands stroked the material lovingly. We'd never had anything like these in our old village. We carried our new skirts, blouses, sweaters, and overcoats up to our rooms and hung them in the closets. Then we girls stood and admired our new apparel. We felt like royal princesses.

Soon our Hong Kong relatives arrived to take us on a tour of the city.

Uncle Tin said, "I'm so happy that all of you are here. Today we'll take you up to Victoria Peak. Then you can see all of Hong Kong and the areas nearby. You'll always remember this place after you have seen it. So follow us."

Our relatives escorted us to a platform where many people were waiting. A big steel car was pulled up next to the platform.

"What do you call this funny car?" I asked.

Baba said, "It's called a trolley car. It's an electric streetcar that will take us places." I was puzzled once again by his answer. We had no cars back in the village.

The trolley took us up to Victoria Peak. I gasped at the breathtaking view. Below we could see Hong Kong Harbor, surrounded by skyscrapers. The sampans looked like tiny dots in the water.

Later, after the tour, we were escorted by our relatives to a fancy restaurant. It was the first time we had eaten in such a fantastic place.

The smiling waitress gave each of us a hot, damp towel to wipe our hands. We ate steamed white rice, succulent roast duck, crackling-skin roast suckling pig, steamed pork patty topped with salted fish, and stir-fried, tender green bok choy.

Wow! We had never eaten like this back in our village. Mama smiled throughout the meal. We all agreed that the meal was "*Ho! Ho!* Very good!"

Our relatives were happy that we were moving to Gold Mountain. They pressed small gifts wrapped in red paper in our hands. They all wished us well by saying, "Have a safe journey."

We enjoyed all the wonderfully new experiences in Hong Kong. But I couldn't help wondering whether Gold Mountain would be like Hong Kong.

"Be very careful when answering questions," Uncle Tin told us. "The officials might trick you. You certainly don't want to be sent back to China in shame."

Now I felt anxious again. I liked this new life already. I didn't want to go back to our old village.

Chapter 9
ABOARD THE SS HOOVER

We all rose early the next morning. Baba said, "Put on your new American outfits today. I don't want you to look like peasants from a backward village."

"Yes, Baba," we replied.

We did as we were told. I felt like a different person, for I was no longer a barefoot country girl. Baba told us that we really looked like Gold Mountain girls. I didn't know what Gold Mountain girls looked like, but I hoped that he was right.

My sisters and I smiled at one another and admired our images in the mirror.

Four rickshaws waited for us in front of the hotel. We climbed in and after Baba told the men where to take us, away we went. It was like a small caravan as the strong men pulled the rickshaws through Hong Kong's crowded streets. There were mostly people and rickshaws and very few cars.

The men dropped us off at a huge pier where a big ship was docked.

Large letters were painted on the ship, but I couldn't read the English words. I later learned it was the ship's name:

SS *Hoover.* This gigantic ship looked as large as the lake in front of our village. Busy workers were loading merchandise from the pier onto the ship. I stared at the red, white, and blue flag fluttering in the breeze.

Baba explained that the ship was named after Herbert Hoover, the president of the United States. "It can carry hundreds of passengers across the Pacific Ocean," Baba said.

"Wow," I said in a soft voice. Suddenly I felt afraid. Everything was too new and strange. And now this giant ship added more worries for me.

Will I get lost trying to find my way? Will Li Hong and Lai Wah get lost? Will Mama get lost? I wondered.

Baba saw that I was scared. He knelt down to comfort me. "You'll be fine, Li Keng. I'll be around to see that everything is all right. You four will be in a cabin by yourselves and I'll be in another cabin with some of the men."

Baba's words made me feel better.

After we boarded the SS *Hoover,* a steward escorted us to our cabin in the third-class section. My eyes could not believe the wonderful sight. The compartment was very clean, with a round porthole, two bunk beds, a wall washbasin, electric lights, and a toilet. The top bunk beds had guardrails. Mama decided that Li Hong and Lai Wah would use the top beds and she and I would use the bottom beds. Lai Wah shouted, "I want to try my bed!" and she scrambled to the top bunk.

Li Hong copied Lai Wah and climbed to the other top bunk. Mama bounced gently on her bunk. She smiled in approval.

"I like this!" I announced to everyone. The ship seemed like heaven.

I especially liked the flush toilet. The hotel in Hong Kong had the same type of toilet. I pulled the cord and the water came rushing down to make a noisy flush. It was like a new toy. At home in the village, we used an outhouse, which had no flush toilet. Each family in the village had an outhouse of its own. The outhouses were grouped together a short distance from the homes. No one had a bathroom inside their house.

At last it was time for us to depart Hong Kong. The SS *Hoover* rumbled and slowly eased away from the dock. We could feel the vibrations in our cabin.

Soon we were at sea. Baba said, "We'll sail across the Pacific Ocean for many days before we get to San Francisco, California."

"How many days, Baba?" I asked.

"Oh, about nineteen days," he replied.

Nineteen? That sounded like a very long time to me.

Each day on board the ship we explored our deck with Baba. Each morning there was a head count of all the passengers. Baba explained, "They do a head count to make sure everyone is safe. Accidents can happen on board. Passengers can accidentally fall overboard."

Our Chinese room attendant served breakfast each morning. He usually brought us hot toast dripping with butter, some fruit, and hot tea or milk. Butter was another thing we had never tasted. We'd never had cow's milk to drink, either.

Li Hong and Lai Wah ate with gusto. Mama and I ate very little, for we were too seasick most of the time to stomach the food. The greasy butter made me gag and I couldn't swallow the cold milk. Mama and I lost weight while Li Hong and Lai Wah filled out nicely.

During the calm days when I wasn't seasick, Baba guided us around and we watched the activities aboard the ship. We saw people playing shuffleboard games and from the railing we watched the waves ebb and flow. We talked to one another about the vastness of the Pacific Ocean. The world seemed so big and I felt so small.

Chapter 10
CROSSING THE PACIFIC

We sailed to Shanghai, to Japan, to Honolulu, Hawaii, and finally to San Francisco. Shanghai and Japan were blurs in my mind, but I could never forget Hawaii. While the ship was docked in Honolulu, I peered over the railing. Dark-skinned young men waved and crooked their fingers for us to throw coins into the water.

Baba said, "Here are some American coins. Throw the money in the water. The water is very deep. The men will dive to the ocean floor to pick up your coin. Then they'll surface to show you the coins. Their big smiles mean 'thank you'."

Baba gave us each a quarter and we took turns tossing the coins. I watched as the divers dove deep into the ocean. Then they shot out of the water, held the coins up, and smiled at us. We three sisters clapped our hands with joy.

As the SS *Hoover* set sail again, the Hawaiian natives shouted, "Aloha! Aloha!"

I asked, "What does 'Aloha' mean, Baba?"

"It means 'good-bye,'" Baba answered. "It also means 'hello.'"

I waved and yelled back, "Aloha!"

The leg of the journey from Honolulu to San Francisco took another four days. All of us were growing more and more excited because San Francisco would be our final stop.

On November 27, 1933, the SS *Hoover* finally entered San Francisco Bay. We didn't sail under the Golden Gate Bridge because the bridge was not built until 1937.

We gathered all our belongings and assembled on deck. As I stood there, the thousands of blinding lights from San Francisco and other cities around the bay were like fireflies in the dark sky. Baba said, "Bundle up in your new coats because November is cold. The San Francisco Bay area is not like our village around this time of the year. Back in Goon Do Hung, the weather is still warm and muggy. Are you warm enough in your coats?"

"Yes, Baba," we replied.

We were told to disembark. Baba pulled us aside and spoke in a low voice. "You four will be staying on Angel Island. Angel Island is the place where new Chinese immigrants are detained. Remember what I told you? The United States passed a law in 1882 called the Chinese Exclusion Act to keep Chinese from coming into the country. The government said the Chinese were taking jobs away from white people. That is why the officials are going to ask you all those questions.

"I won't go to Angel Island because I'm not a new immigrant," Baba went on. "I'll go straight home across the bay to Oakland tonight."

I swallowed hard. We were going to a strange place without Baba.

"Girls, do not forget to call your mother 'Yee,'" Baba told

us. "Do the best you can and I'll be sending something for you to enjoy."

I repeated what Baba said one more time to Li Hong and Lai Wah. "Remember, call Mama 'Yee.' We don't want to be deported back to China!"

Everyone who was new to the western part of the United States was transferred by a small boat called a tender to Angel Island, the "Ellis Island of the West." Ellis Island is in New York, on the eastern coast of the United States. Immigrants from Europe and other points east came through Ellis Island.

Weary and gaunt, holding onto our few meager possessions, we immigrants were herded onto the small boat. Someone instructed us to follow directions, which would be given in our Chinese dialect.

The ride to Angel Island was brief. We were told to follow a guard assigned to us.

Women newcomers were separated from the men. Mama, my sisters, and I followed the guard to the women's barracks.

The guard opened a locked door. I looked around as we stepped inside. We were in a large, rectangular hall with metal cots lined up inside. The windows and doors were barred by chicken wire. Lights hung down from the high ceiling. Despite the lights, the building was dark, bleak, gray, and depressing. I felt as if I were in a prison. Doors were locked shut with guards standing outside.

I turned my mouth downward and frowned. Mama, Li Hong, and Lai Wah kept quiet. I didn't like being locked up. But as scared as I was, I didn't utter a word.

There were about six women in the barracks. How long had they been here? They didn't say anything to us at first.

There were no other children except us three.

The women spoke the same dialect as we did. That helped us greatly. They smiled and asked for the name of our village and our surname. Mama answered them graciously.

That same night all the women ate supper in a separate dining room from the men. Again I noticed the barred doors, barred windows, and drab surroundings. The guards stood and watched us closely as we ate rice, green vegetables, and pork. We were too frightened to enjoy our first meal of Chinese food in Gum Saan.

On the first night, the women who had been on Angel Island for some time told us that some people committed suicide rather than face the shame of being deported back to China. Li Hong, Lai Wah, and I shivered as we listened to the women's tales.

By eight o'clock, we were told to go to the bathrooms to wash up for bed. The toilets were in a different part of the island.

It was dark, so I couldn't see much of the island. The bathrooms were a brief walk from the sleeping compound. We washed quickly and quietly, splashing ourselves with cold running water. Then we dashed back to the barracks. Our metal cots had thin mattresses and dull green blankets. Lights went out by nine o'clock.

In the strange, scary darkness, I wondered what tomorrow would bring.

Chapter 11

LOCKED UP

Not one of us slept well the first night on Angel Island. On the morning of November 28, 1933, we woke up to the sound of a bell.

Someone said, "Get up!"

Dressing quickly, we dashed out of the door as the guard unlocked it. Scrambling toward the bathroom facilities, we blew on our hands to warm up. Angel Island was freezing at that time of year.

The weather here made me think about the warm days in our village, Goon Do Hung. The cold water raised goose pimples down our spines. All of us moved quickly toward the dining compound for breakfast. Luckily, the delicious Chinese *jook* warmed our bodies and satisfied our hunger pangs.

"The Chinese cooks here are not bad," I said. People nodded in agreement.

After breakfast we were herded back to the women's barracks. Again the door locked with a loud click. Again a guard stood outside and watched us with a sour look on his face. He gave me the impression that he didn't like us Chinese people.

There wasn't anything for us to do inside the barracks.

There were no books or games to occupy our time. There were no other children around our ages. The women spent the time talking to one another about their lives in southern China. We talked about our hopes for a better future in Gum Saan.

"I hope to become a teacher of young children some day," I told everyone. Mama smiled at me.

Restless, I got up from my cot and went over to stand in front of the barred windows. I gazed at the scenery and wished Li Hong, Lai Wah, and I could play outside instead of being locked up. Detainees who had been at Angel Island a long time were allowed to go out once a week. Since we were new, we could not go outside.

Suddenly, after lunch, Mama and we girls were called to go to a meeting of a Board of Special Inquiry. Present were one white inspector, one white stenographer, and one Chinese interpreter. We were relieved that one of the officials spoke Chinese and could understand us, as Baba had promised.

Lai Wah hung on to Mama's hand. Li Hong and I fidgeted. We didn't know what was expected of us. We were nervous.

Mama was sworn in. Li Hong, Lai Wah, and I weren't because we were too young. We were instructed to tell the truth. The interpreter explained to us that lying under oath was called perjury. He informed Mama that there was a serious penalty for lying under oath.

First they asked for our names and we answered clearly.

Mama put a mark on the paper as her signature. The interpreter didn't ask Mama whether she could read and write Chinese. She would have written her Chinese name. Li Hong wrote her name in Chinese. Lai Wah and I weren't asked to sign. I kept quiet. I didn't want anyone to fuss over me. Besides, I was scared.

There weren't too many questions, and the hearing didn't take long. The officials just asked for our names and the name of our village. They looked us over carefully. Then we were dismissed from the boardroom. There would be no further inquiry on that day.

We felt relieved, but before we left the room, the Chinese interpreter told us, "We'll call you again soon."

I was concerned for Li Hong. Would she remember the details from the coaching papers? And what if I made a mistake? What if the officials found out that I was lying?

So many things could go wrong.

Chapter 12
A Sweet Surprise

It was very hard not knowing when we would be called again for questioning. There wasn't anything to do to pass the time. Time moved as slowly as a walking turtle and I became bored. I didn't like being locked up.

"I want to go outside, Mama," I said in a soft voice.

Mama pulled us to a quiet corner of the barracks and whispered to us. She didn't want the other women to hear our conversation. We were afraid they might tell the officials about our concerns.

"Don't worry too much, girls. None of us wants to be locked up. But everything will turn out well. Li Keng, I know you want to go outside and look around. You can't. So you might as well make the best of it. Li Hong, do the best you can when they ask you questions. Li Keng, don't fret. Lai Wah, you are probably too young to be questioned much. Now let us think about some good things. We are now on Gum Saan soil. Can you imagine what our relatives and friends are thinking back home in our village?

"Our family is only the second family from Goon Do Hung to immigrate to Gold Mountain. Your Baba has good foresight to bring us here. He wants us to have a better life. He feels that our village isn't a good place for us to live because it is poor and backward and holds no future for us. Now, cheer up and let's chat with the other ladies."

What Mama said made sense. We joined the other women. While we were talking, the door clicked open. We couldn't believe it when an official walked toward Mama and handed her a box.

"What is it, Yee?" I asked, careful not to call her Mama.

It was a box of fresh fruit. We stared in surprise at the plump oranges and apples. The apples were cut in half. Mama thanked the official in Chinese and the official curtly nodded.

"See, I told you that things would get better. Your Baba promised that he would send us something and he remembered." Mama was smiling as she said this.

"Yee, let's share the fruits with everyone," I suggested. "We have enough, don't we?"

"Yes, we do, Li Keng," Mama said. "You're very thoughtful to think of others."

We handed out the split apples and oranges. Everyone ate with relish because the oranges quenched our thirst. The crispy apples, sweet and delicious, were also eaten quickly. It was like a party that afternoon. The fruit lifted our spirits.

For a little while I forgot my concerns about the questions that were to come. I silently thanked Baba for his love for us.

Chapter 13
YEE'S INTERROGATION

We didn't know it, but while we were enjoying the oranges and apples, Baba was being interrogated by the officials. He made two trips to Angel Island during our stay, but he couldn't contact us while we were detained. He could only send us the fruit.

There was no interrogation for Mama and us girls on November 29 or 30.

"How come they haven't called us again, Yee?" I asked. I always remembered to call Mama "Yee" in front of the other women in our barracks. So far, Li Hong, Lai Wah, and I hadn't forgotten once in this matter. I was very proud of my sisters and myself.

"Li Keng, the immigration officials have days off. They need to rest. I'm sure we'll be called again soon," Mama answered.

Mama was right, for on the first of December, she was called to the boardroom again. She was kept there for most of the day. We three sisters stayed in the barracks and kept each other company. I gazed out the barred windows and wished once again to be freed from this jail-like place. I worried about

Mama. Why was she being kept so long? Was she able to answer the hundreds of questions?

In the afternoon, Mama finally came back with a big smile on her face. We ran toward her.

"Girls, I'm finished! I know because I signed the papers with my mark. I'm so relieved," she announced.

I asked Mama, "How did the interrogation go? Were you scared? Did the officials try to trip you up? It took so long. I was really worried."

"I think I did well," Mama replied. "The white officials asked many, many questions about our family. They asked if I was Baba's wife. They asked if you three girls were my daughters. They asked about Baba's family. It was a good thing that I studied the coaching papers and memorized the details back home. Don't worry, Li Keng. Things will be all right. Tomorrow they may call for you girls. Now go and play quietly in the corner. I need a little rest before dinner."

"Yes, Yee, thank you for telling us," I said. "We feel better now," I said. But a feeling of dread still hung over me about what was ahead.

Chapter 14

QUESTIONS FOR LI HONG

Late in the afternoon of that same day, an official called Li Hong to the boardroom. Li Hong fidgeted and looked at Mama with a worried expression on her face.

"It's all right, Li Hong. Do the best you can. The Chinese interpreter will help you. Don't be afraid to ask him to explain to you what you don't understand. Go now." Mama encouraged Li Hong the best way she knew how.

Li Hong stayed in the boardroom until closing time.

"I hope Li Hong does well," I told Mama. "She really tried hard to memorize the coaching papers when we were back in the village."

Li Hong came back about five o'clock. She smiled at us and Lai Wah ran to her.

"How did it go, Li Hong?" Mama asked in a gentle voice.

"I guess I did all right. I remembered most of the answers," Li Hong replied.

The next day, December second, Li Hong's interrogation resumed. She seemed less fidgety this time as she followed the official out of the barracks.

"Do your best, Li Hong!" I called after her.

Li Hong was gone about two hours that morning. I fretted as I sat on the cot, waiting for her to come back. To pass the time I chatted with Mama and Lai Wah about life back in our village.

We were happy to see Li Hong come back with a tiny smile on her face.

"I'm done! I signed my name on the paper," she announced proudly.

Mama smiled and said, "Come, girls, we'll go to the corner to talk."

We moved to a corner of the big room out of earshot of the other women. Mama didn't want them to overhear our conversation.

"How did it really go, Li Hong?" Mama asked anxiously.

"I think I did all right. I didn't remember a few answers, but I did tell them that you were our Yee."

"Don't worry about that now, Li Hong. You did well. They're finished with you. I'm glad your interrogation is over."

Mama patted Li Hong gently on the shoulder. I smiled at Li Hong for her bravery. I knew they would call me next. I would try to be brave, too.

Chapter 15
My Turn

Lunchtime came and I ate without tasting the food. Thoughts raced through my mind. Would the officials call me after lunch? Would I remember the answers to the questions?

Soon after we returned to the barracks, an immigration official yelled out my name.

"Gee Li Keng! Gee Li Keng!"

My eyes darted to Mama and I gave her a quivering smile. Don't let me trip up! Don't let me trip up! I thought.

Mama smiled back and looked at me intently. "Li Keng, you'll do well. I know you can do it. Don't worry so much. Now go! Good luck!"

Three men waited for me in the boardroom, two of them white and one Chinese. One white man was in charge and the other sat at a strange machine. He pushed down keys to take notes. I had never seen a typewriter before. The Chinese man was the interpreter. I felt better when I saw him. The interpreter spoke to me and gestured for me to sit. Then he instructed me to tell the truth.

He asked, "Do you understand, Gee Li Keng?"

I nodded. "Yes, I do."

I concentrated on my replies to the first general questions. I tried not to stumble as I spoke.

"I'm seven years old and attended school for one year. My mother died in the early part of 1933. My purpose for coming to the United States is to attend school. I plan to live in the United States in the years to come."

Then the questions got harder.

"How many wives has your father ever had?"

"Two."

"Is either of your father's wives living?"

"No."

"Were you born to your father's first or second wife?"

"His second wife."

"Where is your mother?"

"She is dead."

"When did she die?"

"She died in the third month of this year, 1933."

"Did you attend your mother's funeral?"

"Yes."

"Who is the woman here with you in this station?"

"She's my Yee."

"Where did your mother die?"

"In our house in Goon Do Hung."

The questioning stopped. I wasn't in the boardroom very long. The interpreter said, "Gee Li Keng, we are finished with you. You may go back to the barracks."

Dashing back to our quarters, I smiled a big smile at Mama, Li Hong, and Lai Wah.

"I'm so happy!" I announced loud enough for everyone in the room to hear. "They're finished with me. I signed the paper with my Chinese name, Yee. I think I did well."

I hoped what I said was true.

Chapter 16

GOOD-BYE TO ANGEL ISLAND

On the next day, December 2, 1933, the guard opened the door and crooked his finger for Mama, Li Hong, Lai Wah, and me to follow him.

We nervously entered the boardroom again. The inspector, the stenographer, and the interpreter waited for us to be seated. We four focused our eyes on the interpreter.

"We have just a few more questions to ask all of you. Don't be nervous. Let me talk to Gee Lai Wah first, all right?"

The interpreter's voice was gentle. We all nodded in reply.

Lai Wah, almost three years old, was bright, friendly, and outgoing. She responded to the interpreter with a big smile and sparkling eyes.

He looked at Lai Wah and asked pleasantly, "Little girl, what is your name, please?"

Lai Wah retorted, "If you don't tell me your name, why should I tell you my name?"

Mama gasped. Li Hong and I exchanged glances. Lai Wah's reply had been honest and natural. She was just a little girl. But would the officials think she was very rude?

The interpreter translated Lai Wah's reply into English for

the inspector and stenographer. Both men roared like lions with their loud laughter. The interpreter joined in, "Ha, ha, ha!"

Mama, Li Hong, and I smiled. We felt wonderful. The tension we had felt a few moments earlier disappeared.

Little sister Lai Wah's quip had cinched the decision for the officials to allow us to stay in the United States. Hooray!

We watched the inspector, a big smile still on his face, stamp our papers.

The interpreter grinned as he translated into Chinese. "Good news! You are released to go today. We'll notify your Baba. He'll meet you in San Francisco to escort you across the bay to Oakland. I'm happy for you. Welcome to Gum Saan. Now go back to the barracks with the guard and gather your things. You'll be escorted to the pier to wait for your departure to San Francisco. Good luck!"

Mama said politely, "Thank you very much for interpreting for us. We're grateful for your help."

The four of us couldn't believe what we had just heard. We were free to leave Angel Island and wouldn't be deported back to China! We could leave as soon as we gathered our things.

Mama, Li Hong, Lai Wah, and I flew back to the women's barracks. The guard must have known by looking at our happy faces that we were leaving. He nodded, but not in an unfriendly manner, as he unlocked the door for us. He really wasn't mean after all.

The other detainees in the barracks stared at us. One lady spoke: "Are you free to go?"

Mama, Li Hong, Lai Wah, and I nodded. "Yes, yes," Mama said. "We're being released today. Oh, we're so happy and so lucky. You ladies have been very kind to us by helping us overcome the strangeness of Gum Saan. The Gee family thanks you. We hope that all of you will be released soon."

"You were here for only one week," one woman said. "That is a record. Some people have been here for weeks and months. Good luck to all of you. Have a good life in the United States. Good-bye."

We gathered our few clothes and toiletries, shoving them into two small suitcases. Another guard waited for us outside the barracks. He escorted us to the pier, where the tender was waiting. As I walked over the wooden planks, I turned and looked back.

"Yee, I'm so happy to leave this jail. Angel Island is terrible," I complained to Mama. "It is no place to put newcomers to Gum Saan."

Mama hushed me and yanked my arm to keep up with her. She gave me a frown.

The tender ferried us over choppy waters to a large pier in San Francisco. We disembarked and saw Baba standing next to a yellow taxicab. He waved and shouted, "Good! Good! Come! Come!"

When we reached Baba, I told him, "Baba, we won't be deported back to China. You must write a letter back to our village and tell Cousin Soe and Paw Paw that we made it to Gold Mountain! We're free! We're free!"

Chapter 17

FERRY TO FREEDOM

Flushed with excitement and happiness, Li Hong, Lai Wah, and I gazed curiously at the waiting yellow cab. This would be our first ride in an automobile.

"Come, climb in," Baba said. "Yee and you girls will sit in the back. One of you will sit in the pullout seat, and I'll sit in front with the driver. There is enough room to squeeze in the two pieces of luggage as well. This cab will take us to the ferryboat."

A ferryboat? I didn't know what Baba was talking about. But for once I didn't ask any questions.

Baba, ever careful, called Mama "Yee" while in the cab. He didn't want anything to jeopardize our entry to Gold Mountain. He would only call her Mama in private.

The taxi wove in and out of traffic. It was a short ride to the ferry. The ferry was a type of boat, but it didn't look like the SS *Hoover.* The steamship was much bigger and didn't carry cars.

I saw many automobiles already parked inside the ferry-boat. Our taxi driver drove slowly and carefully onto the ramp, pulled up behind another car, and braked. Then he stopped the engine and pulled out the key.

Another car followed our taxi. Soon the ferryboat was jammed full with vehicles. A big, strong man pulled a heavy chain across the end of the boat. We were ready to cross the bay to Oakland. Our first ride on a ferry!

"We don't have to stay inside the taxi," Baba said. "I'll escort you four to the upper deck so you can see this magnificent San Francisco Bay. Besides, the fresh air will make you feel good."

The taxi driver also got out of the car and joined us as we climbed to the upper deck. Baba carried on a conversation with the driver in English. The four of us looked at the panoramic view of San Francisco and the East Bay cities. Baba pointed toward the Berkeley hills. "Do you see that tall building?" he asked. "It is the famous campanile, a bell tower, of the University of California in Berkeley. Someday I hope some of you will attend this great university."

"Baba, we will love living here in Gold Mountain," Mama said.

"We four ladies better learn English quickly," Lai Wah said. She was very sharp for a girl not quite three years old.

We all beamed at her for her remark. Baba translated what Lai Wah had said to the taxi driver. The taxi driver nodded and smiled at all of us. He was a nice man.

The ride across the bay took twenty minutes. As the ferry plowed along, some people read newspapers and some dozed. Others walked and talked on the deck.

Soon Baba glanced at his watch. He signaled that it was time for us to get back into the taxi and prepare to disembark. Anxious and excited, we three girls clapped our hands. "I can't wait to get to Oakland!" I said.

The cars ahead of us moved slowly and carefully off of the ferry and onto the pier. Our taxi followed. Baba gave directions and the address to the driver. "Please take us to 723 Webster Street."

The taxi driver quickly maneuvered through the traffic. I saw Chinese faces everywhere, just like ours. That made me feel comfortable.

The taxi stopped in front of a store with the number 723 painted on the front window.

The driver got out and quickly deposited our two pieces of luggage on the sidewalk. He stood there as Baba handed him the charge.

"Thank you, sir. Ladies, welcome to the United States of America!" the taxi driver said in English.

"Say thank you to him in Chinese," Baba told us. "I'll translate."

"*Daw jeh,*" the four of us chorused.

But I was already wondering: Would the people of Gold Mountain welcome us, too?

Chapter 18

WELCOME TO CHINATOWN

I looked down at the sidewalk and frowned.

Baba saw my unhappy look. "What's the matter, Li Keng?"

"Someone back in our village told me the streets were paved with gold. They aren't and I'm very disappointed," I answered.

Baba, being wise and patient, said, "Li Keng, the sidewalks are paved with *do ga nai,* concrete. I'm sorry that you were misled."

He changed the subject to distract me. "Everyone, look over there. See that street? It's Seventh Street. That other street is Eighth Street. Webster Street crosses both Seventh and Eighth. We call Webster Street the heart of Oakland's Chinatown."

While we were standing there on the sidewalk, two men walked toward us. "Congratulations!" one man called to Baba. "Your family finally made it. Welcome to Gum Saan!"

He spoke in Chinese and our faces blossomed with smiles at the warm greeting. I shouldn't have worried about any unkind reception. We felt right at home in Chinatown already.

"Come, let's step inside the store and put our things away," Baba told us.

We stepped inside and looked around. I didn't see any fruits or vegetables at all. The shelves were almost bare except for a few rolls of toilet paper, packets of paper bags, and some cooking utensils. This didn't look like a grocery store to me. It didn't look like the markets back in China.

Baba cleared his throat. "This isn't really a grocery store," he explained. "It is a gambling place that sells lottery tickets. Oakland doesn't allow gambling so we have disguised it as a market. Customers can come in here to buy lottery tickets and hope to win some money. We aren't the only gambling place in Chinatown. There are a number of them scattered around."

Mama and my sisters had puzzled looks on their faces. I knew I did, too. We had only known that Baba was working. He'd never told us about running a lottery store.

I couldn't understand this. Gambling was against the law? Then why was Baba doing it? He was a good man. I was shocked by this information. I thought the others were, too.

"Right now the United States is in the Depression," Baba went on. "Many people are out of work. Businesses aren't doing well, so they're not hiring workers. Many families don't have money to pay rent or to buy food. It is especially hard for Chinese people to find work. So I created a job for myself in order for us to survive. I really don't want to break the law, but what choice do I have?"

We understood what Baba was saying. But just like lying to the officials at Angel Island, breaking the law was scary. Would Baba be arrested by the police officers? Would they arrest us, too?

Baba continued, "Since the store has so much room, I thought we could live here instead of renting another place. I

don't have much money now because I used most of what I
had saved to bring you four to Gum Saan. I hired carpenters
to partition the store into four big rooms."

Mama, Li Hong, Lai Wah, and I looked around again.
"This first room is for our Chinese lottery business," Baba
said, pointing. "The second room is the bedroom for you girls.
The third room is for Mama and me. The last room is the
kitchen, where we have a gas burner. The toilet is at the end
of the hall by itself. We don't have a regular bathroom, but I
had the plumbers install a freestanding tub at the far side of
the kitchen. We'll hang curtains there to give us privacy. We
can take baths any time we want as long as we lock the
kitchen door. You'll brush your teeth over the kitchen sink.
How do you like it so far?"

"We like it very much!" all four of us answered.

It was true. This store was so much grander than our tiny
hut back in Goon Do Hung village. There we had to bring
water inside in pails. We had no indoor toilet. We didn't have
four rooms. There was no comparison to this luxury.

Then Baba, in a serious tone, added quietly, "Mama can't
be seen or sleep at the store for a week or two. If the immigration officials see Mama in our home, they'll surely suspect that
we lied to them. You know that Mama entered Gold
Mountain as my sister and not as my wife. We have to continue the deception."

All of us nodded. "We must not make any mistakes," Baba
went on. "We definitely don't want to be deported back to
China. So Mama will sleep at a cousin's house for the next
week or two. Lai Wah will go with her to keep her company.
When I think the coast is clear, I'll bring Mama and Lai Wah

back here. Meanwhile Li Hong and Li Keng will stay here."

I puzzled over what Baba said, but in the end it made sense to me. Li Hong and Lai Wah also understood the reason behind this temporary arrangement. The fear of deportation hung over our heads like a big, black cloud. How long would we have to live like this? When could we be a real family?

Chapter 19
A Small Celebration

Baba knew that we girls were worried about Mama's status and about our illegal lottery business. He put on a brave smile and said, "I'll order a special dinner from a Chinese restaurant, for we're too tired to cook tonight. We need to celebrate our safe journey to Gold Mountain and being reunited as a family. All of us must remember today's date: December 2, 1933."

Baba wanted us to forget our problems for a short while, and we really appreciated his kindness.

He ordered enough Chinese food for five famished people. The meal arrived within thirty minutes. The deliveryman carried the dinner on a wooden tray balanced on his head. His hands gripped the tray to steady it. He gently put the tray on our dining table.

Our eyes bulged as we smelled the aroma of string beans with beef slices, diced chicken cubes mixed with cashew nuts and snow peas, and *yuke bang*—steamed pork patties covered with chunks of salted fish. A big bowl of steamed white rice, five rice bowls, and five pairs of chopsticks came with the meal. We hadn't had a meal like this since we left Hong Kong. Baba paid the man with a one-dollar bill.

We didn't have any dishes to wash because the restaurant sent a worker to retrieve all the plates and return them to the restaurant. What a treat! After dinner we sat in the kitchen and relaxed. Finally Baba said, "I'll escort Mama and Lai Wah to our cousin's place. It's only three blocks from the store. I'll return soon. So, Li Hong and Li Keng, clean up and get ready for bed. Choose your own beds, and Li Keng, don't you boss Li Hong around. I know you like to tell people what to do. If you are asleep by the time I return, I'll check up on you and see you in the morning. Say good night to Mama and Lai Wah."

Baba, Mama, and Lai Wah left. Mama took a few changes of clothing for herself and Lai Wah. I hoped they could return in a week or two. Would the immigration officials really come to our store and check on us? I was scared.

There were three single beds in the girls' room. They had matching blankets, pillows, and mattresses. More luxury! Our beds in China had been flat wooden boards on top of saw-horses.

I remembered that Baba wanted me to be nice to Li Hong. So I asked, "Li Hong, which bed do you want? Go ahead, you choose first." Li Hong, as sweet as ever, smiled and replied, "I'll take the one in the middle." I bounced on the one next to the wall and then chose that one.

As I lay in my bed, I thought about how fortunate we were to have come such a long way in such a short time. We had left China in early November of 1933. Only one month had passed.

I also smiled to myself for being kind to Li Hong. I hadn't whined once since we left our Goon Do Hung village. Maybe I was growing up.

Before I fell asleep, I prayed to Quan Yin, the Goddess of Mercy. Quan Yin would keep us safe.

Chapter 20
Exploring Our New Home

Li Hong and I both fell into a deep sleep very quickly because we were exhausted from the day's exciting events. It seemed as though we had barely closed our eyes when Baba knocked on our bedroom door and called, "Li Hong! Li Keng! Are you awake yet? Breakfast is ready."

"All right, Baba," we both answered.

It was rather strange to have Baba taking care of us instead of Fung or Mama in China. I wished Mama and Lai Wah were here with us. Li Hong and I missed them already.

We jumped out of bed, changed into day clothes, and walked into the kitchen. Baba scooped *jook* into three bowls. He knew that we needed something familiar for our first Saturday in Gum Saan.

Li Hong and I slurped the *jook* as if we hadn't eaten for days. Then we had second helpings.

After breakfast Baba said, "I'll show you two around Chinatown and have you meet our friends and neighbors. How would you like that?"

Baba introduced us to the Tsang family and the Lee family living next door to us. They all greeted us courteously by saying, "*Foon Ying! Foon Ying!* Welcome! Welcome!" Then we walked to other stores and met more people.

Again these neighbors greeted us with big smiles. "Good! We welcome you to America." Their warm greetings made us feel at home.

We met the owners of a candy store at the corner of Eighth and Webster Streets. The owners had the same last name as ours, Gee. I asked, "Are we cousins?"

Mr. Gee replied, "We may be, but our village is in another district in China. However, we can be cousins, okay?" He asked our names.

"I'm Li Hong," Li Hong said. "She is my younger sister, Li Keng."

I was so proud of Li Hong because she spoke up. Usually I did the talking for both of us.

We continued to explore the block with Baba. We saw a barbershop on Seventh Street. On Franklin Street we were surprised to see three hamburger places operated by white men. Both Chinese people and white people were eating there. They waved to us as we passed by.

On Eighth Street there were more restaurants, grocery stores, and a dry goods store. All the stores on Eighth Street were owned by Chinese merchants. Everyone spoke Chinese to us, and some said "hello" in English.

Baba said, "Soon you'll know everyone and they'll know you."

"Baba," I said, "I'm so glad that we are living in China-town. I don't feel out of place at all. But I know we must still keep up the lie about Mama. I still worry that Li Hong or Lai Wah may make a slip. I'll remind them often."

The Chinese community knew "Yee" was our Mama. Baba told us that our neighbors would keep this a secret.

They were all our friends.

Chapter 21
Back to School

The first weekend flew by quickly. Li Hong and I had fun exploring the shops across the street by ourselves. There was a barbershop along with three restaurants and a laundry.

After dinner on Sunday Baba said, "Tomorrow is Monday and I must enroll both of you at your new school. When we get there, you must remember to tell them that you have a father, but no mother."

Li Hong and I nodded.

"You'll like Lincoln Grammar School because the teachers are very good," Baba told us. "Many of the students are Chinese and they speak Chinese. If you don't understand the English, you can always ask someone to help you. Don't be afraid to ask for help. Obey your teachers and pay close attention. Try to learn something new every day."

"Li Hong and I will study hard, Baba. Don't worry about us," I said.

My sister added, "We will learn how to read and write English."

Monday morning arrived. Baba escorted us to the school right after breakfast. Again he reminded us, "Your mother died in China. You entered the United States with my sister, your 'Yee.' You will do well in school. The teachers will help you and I'll help you at home."

My sister and I were assigned to different classes. I was assigned to a second-grade class and Li Hong was assigned to a third-grade class. "You know the way back to the store by now," Baba told us. "Lunch will be ready for you at twelve o'clock. There is no food for students here. See you two later." He waved and left.

A lady escorted Li Hong to her classroom and the Chinese lady led me to a second-grade class. The white teacher greeted me with a big smile and I gave her a nod. She said something to me, but I didn't understand a word. I stood by the door without moving. My heart thumped loudly in my chest. I hoped the teacher couldn't hear it.

Soon a Chinese boy entered the classroom. The teacher whispered to him and he immediately translated what she had said. "The teacher wants you to sit down on that chair. Don't be afraid." He gestured to a chair near the front of the room and motioned for me to sit. I did. It was a big relief.

Soon the nine o'clock bell rang for classes to begin. More students filed in quietly and in an orderly manner. I noticed there were a number of Chinese children, a few white children, and a few Japanese children.

The teacher greeted everyone with a big smile. She went to the blackboard and wrote my name, Li Keng Gee. She put my family name last, because I was in America now. Everyone looked in my direction, but I didn't even smile. I didn't know how to react. My heart went thump, thump again.

Soon the classroom activities started. We all stood up and

faced the flag to say the Pledge of Allegiance. I stood and put my right hand over my heart like the rest of the class. I listened carefully to the words. What a wonderful way to honor the United States, my new country. School here was very different from my school in China.

The two recesses in the morning gave me a chance to meet and mingle with the other students. Most of them spoke our Chinese dialect. I looked for Li Hong on the playground and found her. She said, "I like it here!" I agreed with her.

The teacher taught me how to print my name, the Lincoln School name, and numbers from one to ten. I practiced for a while. It was not hard. I liked this. The lady was so kind and I felt lucky to have her as my teacher.

We went home for lunch. Li Hong and I walked with some other children who also lived in Chinatown. Two girls in the neighborhood, Helen Hong and May Lee, became our friends for life. Both girls were already Americans. Helen was born in Oakland. Her family ran the Man Lung grocery store. May was born in Oklahoma. Her family moved to Oakland's Chinatown at the beginning of the Depression.

Baba greeted us as we walked through the door. "How did your morning go? Have you learned any English words? Have you met any friends?"

"Baba, Lincoln School is good," Li Hong replied.

"I love the school, too!" I said.

Baba beamed. "I'm so happy and proud of both of you. Come, let's have some lunch now." We ate wonton soup, which is like ravioli in broth.

Soon we had to return to Lincoln School for the afternoon session. "Li Hong, I'll wait for you in the playground," I said.

"We can go home together." Li Hong nodded.

In the afternoon we had physical education, a reading lesson, and music. Time passed quickly and we were dismissed at three o'clock.

Li Hong and I had survived our first day at school in Gum Saan. We were very happy that no one even asked us once whether we had a mother. I hoped no one would ever ask.

I wished that Mama and Lai Wah were home. I wanted to share my experiences with them. When would they return?

Chapter 22

HOMECOMING

Every day for the next two weeks I pestered Baba with the same questions. "Baba, have you seen any immigration officials lurking around to check on us? How long must we wait for Mama and Lai Wah to return home? Have you gone to see them?"

Baba tried to be patient with me. My anxiety must have really shown on my face and in my voice.

"Li Keng, you're a pest and you really try my patience. I understand that you're worried and anxious for Mama and Lai Wah to come home. I, too, am concerned. No, I haven't seen any immigration officials in Chinatown. I don't know when Mama and Lai Wah may come home. Yes, I visited Mama and Lai Wah while you two girls were at school. They're enjoying their stay with our nice cousins."

Then Baba looked very, very serious. "I have bad news to tell you girls. Paw Paw died on the way back to her village after she left us at Som Bot City. Our neighbors said she tripped and fell. She died right away. I'm sorry that Paw Paw never learned that we made it to Gum Saan. Mama loved her mother very much. She is really sad about her death."

"Oh no!" I cried. Tears streamed down my face as I sobbed. My dear Paw Paw was no longer alive.

Baba patted my shoulder to show me that he understood my sadness. Li Hong remained quiet and clamped her lips together. Paw Paw's death was like a big cloud of misery hanging over our heads.

Just before the American New Year of 1934 arrived, Baba said in an excited voice, "Girls, I'm going to bring Mama and Lai Wah home. No one in Chinatown has heard or seen any immigration officials. I think the coast is clear. Tomorrow is New Year's Eve and it will be a good day for our family to be reunited again."

Li Hong and I clapped our hands and jumped for joy. I said to her, "Do you want to help me clean up our room? We can sweep the floor and dust the furniture. We can wipe the kitchen table and straighten out our things. When Mama and Lai Wah come home they'll see a clean place. Okay with you, Li Hong?"

I remembered Baba's warning not to boss Li Hong around. I was very pleased with myself and showed Baba that I was an obedient daughter.

On New Year's Eve, Baba walked Mama and Lai Wah back to our store. He carried a small suitcase. Li Hong and I waited anxiously for them. Finally we saw them crossing Webster Street. Li Hong and I dashed to the corner to greet them. "Yee and little sister, welcome home!"

Chapter 23
A New Beginning

The year 1934 arrived with the sun shining through our store windows. During breakfast, Baba said, "Today is the first day of the new year. The United States has a new president and his name is Franklin Delano Roosevelt. I hope he does a good job leading us out of the Depression. When you see people today, say 'Happy New Year' to them. Let's practice saying those three words now. Happy New Year! Happy New Year!"

Lai Wah shouted, "Happy New Year!"

"I'll cook a special American-style dinner tonight to celebrate the new year and the reunion of our family," Baba told us. "We'll have pan-fried pork chops with apple sauce, mashed potatoes with brown gravy, string beans, and vanilla ice cream for dessert. How about it?"

"Yes, yes, Baba!" we all answered. Mama smiled. She looked very happy.

That evening we enjoyed Baba's delicious pork chops. The smooth mashed potatoes smothered with brown gravy brought "yum yum" sounds from us girls. It was the first time we ever had ice cream, too. It was grand.

Then Baba announced, "Li Hong and Li Keng, it's very important for you to know something of our heritage. You two will start attending Chinese school tomorrow after your regular school. I've already enrolled you in a school on Ninth Street. The teacher, Mr. Wong, has a fine reputation and enjoys teaching Chinese children. Chinese school is from four P.M. to six P.M. from Monday to Friday. Saturdays you will go from nine A.M. to noon. I've scraped up four dollars for your tuition."

This was very nice of Baba, we knew. Baba's business wasn't good. Few people could afford to buy lottery tickets. He didn't make much money, even though we kept the store open from nine in the morning until nine at night.

"Thank you, Baba," I said. Li Hong smiled and nodded in agreement. Mama supported Baba's decision by saying, "*Ho! Good!*"

I was already thriving in American school. A lady psychologist tested me in a nonverbal test. She had me draw squares, circles, and rectangles. She asked me to tie two shoestrings and draw a picture of a house. Then she had me trace the fingers of my left hand.

The test was brief. The psychologist scribbled a number on the paper, which was my score. I must have scored well, because I was allowed to stay with my second-grade class.

Li Hong was having difficulties in class. She said that learning was hard for her. The psychologist tested her also and recommended that she be placed in a class for slower learners.

The school sent a letter home to inform Baba. Mama and Baba agreed that the special class would be the right placement for Li Hong. My sister was relieved.

I did well in Chinese school also. Practicing calligraphy was fun. The soft brush dipped in black ink brought Chinese characters to life. I enjoyed learning new characters and memorizing Chinese poetry, too. It offered me a great sense of accomplishment.

Mr. Wong gave me good grades and praised me as I applied myself to mastering the lessons. "You're going to be very successful, Li Keng," he said to me one day. That made me very proud. I wanted to do well in my new country.

Li Hong did not share my enthusiasm for Chinese school. After a few months, Mr. Wong gently suggested that she drop out. Baba and Mama were very disappointed, but they never chided her. She was much happier doing chores at home. She washed our clothes, dusted the furniture, and helped Mama with the cooking.

My sister continued to attend Lincoln School every day. She enjoyed her new class. All the teachers loved her and she had many friends from school and from the neighborhood. And even though Li Hong sometimes had trouble remembering her lessons, not once did she ever make the mistake of calling our mother "Mama." She always remembered to call her "Yee."

Chapter 24
Playing the Lottery

Baba barely made enough money from his lottery business to make ends meet. He had hired a cousin to help in the lottery room. The two men marked the tickets for the customers. Since times were hard, customers played with small amounts of money: nickels, dimes, and quarters.

All day long the customers—mostly Chinese men, but also some white men and a few Filipino men—walked in and out of our store. We had no privacy. But many of these customers became our friends. They often stopped to exchange a few words with Li Hong, Lai Wah, and me. Mama greeted the customers with a big smile and tried out a few words of English. She was able to say, "Hello, how are you?" In time her English improved.

Some days the earnings were fair and some days they were bad. Baba wasn't able to save any money because he had five mouths to feed now. Often I heard Baba and Mama talking about our lack of money. Mama said, "I hope we can do better soon."

Sometimes it seemed as though we'd been better off in China. I worried about our finances, too. I realized that there were times when we didn't have enough money for rent, groceries, clothes, and other expenses. What would happen to us? Would we become homeless? Would we be sent back to China?

If the police department closed our lottery business, we would have no money at all coming in. Baba had no other jobs. Years earlier, he had been a handyman. He had also had a grocery truck that sold groceries to the fraternities and sororities at the University of California in Berkeley. He had only begun in the lottery business a few years before he brought us from China in 1933.

The worst thing about running an illegal gambling business was our fear of being raided by the police. They wanted to close down all the lottery places in Chinatown, not just ours. Sometimes rumors spread through the neighborhood that the police were coming. Then all the lottery places went on alert and shut down for a while. But we weren't always warned.

I was home one day in June for summer vacation. Li Hong and Lai Wah were playing next door. Mama was in the kitchen preparing food. Suddenly I heard the sound of screeching brakes.

I looked out our window to see a police paddy wagon and a group of plainclothes detectives rushing into our store. They carried sledgehammers and axes.

The policemen crashed through the lottery door. Baba and Cousin stood to one side of the room as the detectives destroyed the gambling table, chairs, and tickets. I shook as I watched from the doorway, terrified.

A police officer yelled at Baba and Cousin, "You're operating an illegal business and you're under arrest! You stupid

Chinks go back to China!" Then he put handcuffs on Baba and Cousin.

Baba and Cousin were roughly pushed into the paddy wagon. Before the door slammed behind them, Baba yelled to us, "Don't worry! I'll be home soon!" Then the paddy wagon took off.

I stood there in shock. What would happen to Baba? Would he be sent to jail?

Mama and I both cried as we watched the paddy wagon disappear.

We closed the store immediately. After a few hours Baba and Cousin came home. They had walked home from the police department.

"We're okay," Baba said. "We're out on bail. Our Chinese bail bondsman paid our fines. Don't worry about what happened today. Raids happen to other lottery places, too."

Mama looked glum. I knew the experience had shaken her up. It shook me up, too.

After I went to bed, I tossed and turned all night long. Would our fortune ever improve? Would we be raided again? Where would we get the money to replace the wrecked furniture? Would Baba have to go into even more debt to feed us?

Chapter 25

A New Member of the Family

Although Baba had been released from jail, he looked haggard and worried. He had to close the lottery for a few days and that made us even poorer. He frantically borrowed money from some cousins and replaced the gambling room furniture.

Soon the loyal customers returned and played tickets again. Money slowly trickled back into our cash register.

Mama helped by marking tickets whenever Baba and Cousin went on a break. The customers liked her friendly manner and cheerful smiles. I helped, too. Every day after school, I spread out the tickets and sorted them into piles. At four o'clock, I headed to Chinese school. Baba and Mama were pleased. They said that I was doing the work of an adult.

Life resumed quietly as we went about our daily routines. But we were constantly on alert for another raid by the police. If the police caught me helping in the lottery room, would they handcuff me and haul me to jail in the paddy wagon? I sure didn't want that to happen.

One day in the spring of 1934, I noticed that Mama's stomach was protruding, even though she tried to hide her figure with a large apron.

"Mama, are you going to have a baby?" I asked hopefully.

"Yes, Li Keng, I'm going to have a baby," Mama replied with a smile.

"When is it due?" I asked.

"Sometime in September," Mama said. "I hope this time I'll have a boy. Baba and I want a boy to carry on our Gee family name." She wiped her hands on her apron. "Now go tell Li Hong and Lai Wah."

I quickly spread the good news to my sisters. Lai Wah shouted, "Hooray! We can take care of the baby! Maybe it will be a boy!"

We girls wanted a boy baby, too.

Even though I was happy, I was also worried. How would we have enough money to feed another mouth?

The coming baby caused a new legal problem. Mama had immigrated to the United States as Baba's sister. The new baby could not officially use the Gee family name. The new baby had to be born to legal parents with a proper family name. What were we going to do?

Baba hatched a plan to solve this problem. He was still afraid that the officials might learn that Mama was his wife. He found a man by the name of Sheng Wong who was willing to become Mama's "paper husband."

Baba and Sheng Wong filled out a proper marriage certificate. On paper Mama became Mrs. Sheng Wong, but she still kept her Gee name. Baba paid Sheng Wong a sum of money. Mr. Wong promised to disappear and he did. He kept his word to Baba and Mama, and the baby had a legal last name.

Everyone was happy that we had solved the name problem. But I was still worried. How would Mama and Baba feel if the baby turned out to be a girl? We hoped that Quan Yin, Goddess of Mercy, would grant our family a baby boy.

Chapter 26
A Red Egg Party

Mama waited patiently for the baby to arrive. Her stomach grew larger and larger. She waddled like a duck as she walked.

"You don't have to help in the lottery room anymore, Mama," Baba said. "You must take it easy and rest."

"I don't want to sit around and do nothing," Mama replied. "I'll go visit Mrs. Fong at the Man Lung Grocery Store. The walking exercise will do me good. We'll have a grand time. Her children are about the same ages as ours, so they can play together."

Mama also met up with another Mrs. Gee, whose husband owned a barbershop across the street. The three ladies became fast friends. They gossiped, played a Chinese dominoes game called Pai Gow, and kept their eyes on the children from the three families. We children played well with one another.

The months flew by quickly. Dr. Lam, a doctor midwife, came to check on Mama several times. Dr. Lam spoke English and Chinese. She had delivered many Chinese babies in Chinatown. She charged fifty dollars for Mama's care before and after the birth. Baba paid her in installments. The midwife always smiled and chatted with Li Hong, Lai Wah, and me.

Chinese people believed that mothers must rest for a month after giving birth. So Baba hired Mrs. Young to take care of Mama and the baby after the baby arrived. Mrs. Young was to stay with us for one month.

During the years of the Great Depression, most babies were delivered at home. September 12, 1934, was the big day. Mama quietly told Baba, "I think the baby is coming." Baba called Dr. Lam and Mrs. Young, who both arrived quickly. The two women were ushered into Mama's bedroom and Baba joined them. Dr. Lam wanted Baba to help, too. We three sisters were told by Baba, "Go and play outside. We don't want you to get in the way."

We tried to play hopscotch on the sidewalk, but our minds were on the birth of the baby. We kept our ears turned to Mama's bedroom. Would it be a boy or a girl?

Soon we heard Dr. Lam calling us. We rushed inside to Mama's bedroom. "You have a beautiful little sister!" the doctor said.

Little sister? Oh no! Now we had four girls. We sisters were so disappointed that it wasn't a boy. A boy would have made Baba and Mama very happy. Chinese people especially value sons because boys carry on the family name. But we were glad that Mama and the baby were doing fine.

The baby had lots of dark hair. She weighed about eight pounds.

Dr. Lam finished her work and turned the baby over to Mrs. Young. Dr. Lam told Mama, "Rest up now and try to get some sleep. I'll come back tomorrow morning to check on you and your new daughter."

After the doctor left, we heard Mama cry, "I wanted a boy!"

Mrs. Young soothed her by saying, "Maybe you'll have a boy the next time you become pregnant."

When Dr. Lam came back the next day, Baba and Mama asked her to name the baby. "We don't know many American names for girls," Baba said. "Please do us the honor of naming our new daughter."

Dr. Lam quickly came up with "Nellie." Everyone liked the name because it was easy for Chinese people to pronounce. Later Nellie would receive a Chinese name.

A few days later I overheard Mama say to Mrs. Young, "I wish Li Keng was a boy. Had she been a boy, my life would be fulfilled."

I became sad when Mama said that. She valued me less because I was a girl. But there was nothing I could do about it.

What Mama said added another burden to my shoulders. Why hadn't I been born a boy?

We gave Nellie a Red Egg party when she was one month old. The party, somewhat like a christening, was held at home. We invited relatives, friends, and neighbors to join us in the festivities.

Days before, Baba and Mrs. Young dyed hard-boiled eggs and cooked a big pot of pigs' feet with vinegar, ginger, and brown sugar. They also prepared a large pot of chicken boiled with rice wine and ginger.

On this special day, the eggs, pigs' feet, and chicken were laid out for visitors. Many Chinese people believed that eggs promoted fertility, which meant the mother would have more babies. The pigs' feet would help the mother to produce more milk. The chicken would help her regain her strength after giving birth.

We older sisters helped to get the house ready. Guests dropped in all afternoon. They presented Nellie with *lay see,* money wrapped in red paper. Our new sister brought us much happiness on this day.

Chapter 27

TROUBLES

Nellie's Red Egg party cheered us up for weeks. It was the first party for our family since we entered the United States. The *lay see* money helped buy us food. It also gave us hope.

Mama went back to her job marking tickets in the lottery room. So it was up to us, the three sisters, to take care of the baby when we weren't in school.

Li Hong washed all the diapers in the bathtub. She used her hands and a scrubboard to get the job done. Then she hung the laundry out to dry on a clothesline.

I sterilized all the milk bottles and made the formulas. Lai Wah helped by playing with Nellie and changing diapers. We enjoyed taking care of our new baby.

The lottery business was still doing poorly. Lack of money caused Baba and Mama lots of stress. Baba borrowed more money from cousins. He also asked for credit from three different grocery stores. The amount owed was added up at the end of each month and Baba paid the bills.

One time Baba couldn't pay the bills because he didn't have enough money. I took a grocery list to the third store. The grocer looked at me sadly and said, "Sorry, Li Keng. We can't give your family any more credit. Tell your Baba that we would be happy to do business again if he pays up what he owes us."

I felt so ashamed. I rushed home, clutching the list and weeping. Baba told me, "Go try store number one. They have known me well during all these years. Maybe they will extend our credit for another month."

I wiped my eyes and trudged to store number one. They were very kind, for they extended our credit. "Tell your Baba not to worry about the money," the owner said.

We really appreciated our dinner that night. We had rice, vegetables, and a stir-fry pork dish. We had enough to eat, but nothing fancy.

Friends and relatives rallied to help us. Sometimes we girls were given hand-me-down clothes. Uncle Jin, who was married to Mama's sister, gave us lots of help. Uncle Jin had left his wife in China and had come to Gum Saan by himself. He visited us often on his days off from his laundry business. He always brought food.

Often Uncle Jin went to a Chinese grocery store and had several hundred-pound sacks of rice delivered. Then he quietly slipped some money to Mama.

The rice would last for many months and the money helped Baba settle some of our family's debts. Uncle said, "It is my gift to you and I don't want you to pay me back."

We all said, "Thank you, Uncle," and gratefully accepted his generous gifts. He was our angel.

I wondered what was going to happen to us. Would we ever have enough money?

Chapter 28

ANOTHER CHANCE

By September of 1935, Nellie was one year old and learning how to walk. She was a bright little girl. Lai Wah, who was very responsible now, chased around the store after her. Lottery customers patted Nellie's head and gave her big smiles.

I was loaded with schoolwork and continued to help in the lottery room. That didn't leave me much time for anything else. But I never complained about my lack of time to play because I really wanted to help. Baba often told the customers, "Li Keng does a good job helping here." Wow! To receive a compliment from Baba was well worth the effort to do my best.

Then, in late September, 1935, we three older sisters noticed that Mama's stomach was expanding again. Lai Wah giggled and announced, "Mama is going to have another baby! I hope it's a boy!"

Mama smiled. "Do you think this time it will be a boy?" she asked. "I pray to Quan Yin to grant me my wish. This baby will arrive sometime in January."

The whole family waited anxiously for Mama to give birth. Every night I prayed to Quan Yin, "Please send us a boy."

Baba called Dr. Lam and Mrs. Young to help us again. The baby arrived on January 28, 1936. It was another girl!

Mama and Baba shook their heads sadly. I felt so sorry for them. Quan Yin had not answered our prayers.

Again Baba asked Dr. Lam to give an American name to the baby. Dr. Lam replied, "The most common names for girls these days are Helen, Mary, Shirley, May, and Betty. But how does Leslie sound to you? Leslie can also be a boy's name."

Mama agreed, "I like the sound of Leslie. Maybe I'll have a boy after Leslie. She may bring me good luck." So Leslie it was.

But after Dr. Lam left, I heard Mama cry again to Mrs. Young. "We don't need another girl in our family," she wailed. "Oh dear, I've given Baba four more girls! When will I be able to produce a male heir?"

Mrs. Young answered gently, "Please don't upset yourself. I'm sure someday you'll have a boy. Now close your eyes and get some rest."

One month passed and Leslie also had a Red Egg party. Friends, relatives, neighbors, and a few lottery customers dropped in to meet our new little sister. Leslie received a number of *lay see.*

That night Mama opened the red envelopes and counted up the money. "Baba, we have enough money to pay our rent this month!" Baba broke out in a big grin.

Leslie had brought our family good fortune already!

Chapter 29

LIFE IN CHINATOWN

We had lived in Chinatown for three years now. We had made friends with other Chinese families and we went to Lincoln School with their children.

My friend Helen Hong was one year younger than me. Another friend, May Lee, and I were the same age. With their help, I learned English quickly.

Helen helped at her family's grocery store whenever she had any free time. She attended Chinese school just like May and me. She was smart, had a good ear for languages, was kind to others, and definitely was a leader.

Beautiful May was slender, with large bright eyes and gorgeous smooth skin. She attracted people to her like a magnet. She was indeed a very popular girl. Everyone liked her.

I was really happy attending school with my friends. Each day I learned something new and interesting. The teachers went out of their way to help me with my English. After a while I was able to speak well and was on grade level in other subjects, too. Sometimes I was teased by other children as a "teacher's pet." I loved the teasing.

Once a month our school held an assembly. We walked to the big auditorium, sat on mats on the floor, and watched in awe as our classmates entertained us by singing, playing musical instruments, dancing, and doing skits. Almost always two sisters by the names of Norma and Elfreda Young tap danced for us in glittering costumes. Their graceful bodies moved in time with the rhythm of the music. I thought they seemed like movie stars.

Story time was my favorite part of the day. I loved the tales of Cinderella, the Princess and the Pea, Snow White and the Seven Dwarfs, Peter Rabbit, and many others.

I continued to make good progress in Chinese language school. Mr. Wong kept me interested in Chinese literature. Baba and Mama were happy that I was doing well in both my schools. By now I was in the fourth grade. I was very pleased with myself.

Baba always encouraged me. "Li Keng, work hard and learn as much as you can," he said. "Someday you will go into work that you enjoy. A good education is a must if you want to leave Chinatown and find a good job in the white world. Chinese people who have found better paying jobs outside of Chinatown are looked up to as people of importance."

I was happy to have Baba's support. I told him, "Baba, my goal in life is to become a schoolteacher. I want to leave Chinatown when I'm older." Baba nodded and smiled to show his approval.

I looked forward to Saturday afternoons because I had two hours of free time between twelve-thirty and two-thirty. I could do whatever I wanted before three. That was when I was expected to fold lottery tickets for customers.

"Go to the library and borrow some American books to read," Baba told me. "It's very important for all of us to read. The library is more than a mile each way, so be careful crossing the streets. Watch out for cars."

"Thank you, Baba, I'll check out a few books and bring them home to share with everyone." I knew my eyes sparkled when I said that. I couldn't wait to use the library. There was a library in our school, but I was going to the much bigger one in downtown Oakland. The library was quiet like a hospital. I wanted to spend lots of time there. Going to the library was a special event for me.

What a joy it was to borrow books for free! We didn't have any such thing as a library back in our village in China. There we had no books at all. We didn't even have magazines or newspapers in our village.

Library books took the place of toys in our family. We were so poor that we couldn't afford to buy toys. We sisters never had dolls to play with. We played with empty orange crates and corrugated paper boxes. We cut out paper dolls from newspapers. We found an old rope, which we used to jump rope on the sidewalk in front of our store. We cut up old pillowcases into small squares and sewed them together with rice inside so we could play hopscotch with beanbags. Lots of other children played with us. Did we have fun!

Every Friday afternoon people from the Salvation Army, a religious group, gathered on the corner of Eighth and Webster Streets. They played drums and clanged cymbals as they sang, "Jesus loves me, this I know, 'cause the Bible tells me so."

Some people in the audience understood the words. Some didn't. But everyone enjoyed the music. They thought it was good entertainment.

We didn't worry too much about immigration officials anymore. No one came to check on us. But we still pretended that Mama was our Yee when we were in school.

Chapter 30
GHOSTS

One afternoon in 1937, I ran home from Lincoln School to help in the lottery room as usual. But when I got to the store, I stopped in my tracks.

An Oakland police officer was sitting inside near the front door. What was he doing there? Had something terrible happened to Baba and Mama? Had they been arrested? I was worried because the police officer looked at me and didn't utter a word. He wasn't very friendly.

Baba and Mama came out with long, drawn faces.

"What happened, Baba?" I cried. "Why is this police officer sitting here?" My voice sounded almost hysterical.

Baba pulled me aside. "Calm down, Li Keng," he said. "The officer has been assigned to sit in our store to stop our lottery business. I don't know how long he will stay here. Now come to the kitchen and eat something before you head for Chinese school."

After a small snack I trudged slowly to school. I couldn't pay any attention to my lessons and I didn't want to practice my calligraphy. My stomach kept knotting and my heart was jumping.

At six o'clock I ran back to the store. I had to find out whether the police officer was still there.

This time, there was no police officer. Baba met me at the front door. "The officer left after you went to Chinese school," he said. "But he'll be back tomorrow. He's going to sit here every day this week from nine to four. City Hall wants to close us down."

Mama joined us. In a sad voice she said to Baba, "I hate this lottery business. The girls are getting older now. They need some privacy. We need a place where the lottery customers cannot walk through our living quarters. Please, Baba, find a place where we can relax. Maybe somewhere in the next block. Can you look around?"

I didn't say anything. It was up to Baba and Mama to decide and solve this problem. I didn't know how to find another place to live.

"Let me think about it," Baba said sadly.

The next day he announced, "I just spoke to the store's landlord. He plans to tear down this building and rebuild something more modern. That means our lease will end soon. So I rented an old house just around the corner on Seventh Street. We can use part of the kitchen as the lottery room. The customers can come through the back door. That way they won't have to walk through our living quarters."

I was very glad that we would be moving out of the grocery store. But I knew Baba and Mama really hated running the lottery because it was against the law. Baba couldn't find another job. The Great Depression was still going on, and many people were out of work.

I didn't like our new home, even though it had more rooms

than our old one. It was dark, gloomy, and smelled musty. The floors creaked and I was sure that the house was haunted. No one had lived in this sad-looking house for a very long time.

We all helped by carrying small things to the house. A few of our men friends did the heavy moving work. Part of the kitchen became the lottery work space.

Life continued as usual. Mama helped with marking the tickets. I also helped by folding the tickets. We three older sisters took care of Nellie and Leslie.

One day the police raided us again. Only Baba was in the lottery room this time. Mama was busy doing chores and checking on Nellie and Leslie. The police officer handcuffed Baba and hauled him away in the paddy wagon.

Mama, Li Hong, Lai Wah, and I burst into tears. Nellie and Leslie were frightened. We were all terribly afraid.

Baba came home after he was bailed out by the bondsman. His lottery business was closed again and no money went into the cash register.

I wished I could earn money to help with our family's expenses, but I was only ten years old. What were we going to do?

Then one day Mama got very sick. She ran a fever and coughed day and night. Baba sent for a Chinese herbal doctor to check on her. The doctor prescribed certain herbs to help her get well. Baba boiled the herbs in water. When the liquid was ready, Mama drank the herbal tea. She drank another cup every day for the next three days. Finally her fever went down and her cough was gone. Her energy came back, too. We were really happy to see her well again.

But Mama believed she knew the cause of her illness. She

said, "Baba, this house is unlucky for us all. It seems as if there are ghosts here, even though we haven't seen any. It's dark. It has shadows. We must move to another place. Please, Baba."

We children became even more afraid of the house we had never liked. We said, "Let's move, Baba."

Baba found a flat at 333 Seventh Street, just a few minutes walk from the old house. We moved in with high hopes that it would be a lucky house. We hoped that there would be no ghosts there. I kept my fingers crossed.

Mama couldn't help with the lottery anymore. She had to take care of Nellie and Leslie because we three older girls were at school. She did all the cooking for the family.

That spring, we girls noticed that Mama was pregnant again. We all prayed to Quan Yin for a boy.

Mama gave birth on October 28, 1938.

"You have a beautiful baby girl!" Dr. Lam said with a smile.

Mama couldn't believe what she heard. "No!" she cried. Dr. Lam told her that girls were just as precious as boys. "Do you want to call her Betsy?"

This time I asked Baba if I could name the new baby. "Baba, let's call her Florence after Florence Nightingale, a famous nurse who did lots of good deeds. I read about her in a book. You let Dr. Lam choose names for Nellie and Leslie. Please let me choose now. We girls don't like the sound of Betsy."

Surprisingly Baba and Mama agreed. I sure felt important.

Mama said, "I'm going to give Florence the Chinese name of Ling Oy. No more Li like Li Hong, Li Keng, and Lai Wah. Maybe that will break the jinx of no baby boy. Ling Oy means 'deserving special love.' Does that sound right, everyone?"

We all agreed.

Mrs. Young helped Mama for a month. Mama was so disappointed that she wept on and off for weeks. She sobbed, "I don't want another daughter!" We older girls felt sorry for Mama, but we loved our new baby sister. She was beautiful, with a head full of dark black hair, a light, smooth complexion, and big eyes like Baba's.

Baba became very quiet for a while after Florence was born. He didn't smile as much.

Mrs. Young slept with the five girls in the back bedroom. She told Mama, "I don't feel good in this house. I think there are ghosts here. I can feel them. I'm not afraid, but I thought you should know."

Mama became very frightened. We three older girls were frightened, too.

She said to Baba, "Baba, we must move again after Florence's Red Egg party. Mrs. Young said this place has ghosts. I'm afraid and the girls are also."

Baba agreed to look for another place for us to live.

This time we had to find a lucky house.

Chapter 31

CHANGES

By 1938 we had eight people in our family. Mama had given birth to three girls within five years. We were still poor and always worried about money. But Uncle Jin from San Francisco continued to give us money and sacks of rice. Relatives and friends brought used clothing for us to wear. Our family always felt grateful for their help.

"Baba, when you look for another place, take me with you. I want to check out the place before we rent it," Mama said one day.

Baba searched around the neighborhood and finally found a flat at 725 Harrison Street. Mama went with him to check it out. "I like this place," she said. "It is bright and the rooms are spacious."

Our new home was built in the late eighteen hundreds. Another Chinese family rented the top floor. We rented the street floor, which had five large rooms. Our rent was seventeen dollars a month.

Our flat had no bathroom. The bathtub was upstairs. We had to share it with the other family. Baba hired a plumber to install a free-standing bathtub next to the kitchen. The toilet was outside the back door. It was an outhouse, really. But it was still better than what we had had in China.

The kitchen had a gas stove with four burners. Baba had to borrow money from an association that he belonged to in order to buy a large icebox—people didn't have refrigerators back then. The icebox could hold fifty-pound blocks of ice.

On Fridays the iceman arrived in a big truck with new blocks of ice. The big, strong man hauled the ice blocks and put them in our icebox. We were always glad to see him because he chipped off small pieces of ice for us to eat. It was a special treat on hot summer days and even on cold winter days.

Baba said, "Li Keng, it is your job every morning to empty the pan of water from the melted ice. Don't forget, because if you do, the pan will overflow."

"Oh sure, Baba, no problem," I replied. I always remembered to empty the pan.

We had bunk beds in our girls' bedroom now. The top bunks had guardrails to keep us from falling off. We had only one dresser and that was not enough to hold all our clothes. So we girls used several orange crates and corrugated boxes to hold our things. Dresses and coats were hung on pegs nailed to the door and walls. We didn't mind the crowded conditions. Lai Wah, who was seven years old, said, "This is very cozy." We agreed. Lai Wah was always optimistic.

Our living room had one sofa and one table bought from the Goodwill store. In fact, everything in the house came from Goodwill except the bunk beds. We bought the beds with borrowed money.

Mama and Baba seemed pleased about the new place. After

living there for a while, Mama said, "I don't think there are ghosts here."

We children were happy when we heard that. Now we didn't have to be scared anymore.

Were things finally looking up?

Chapter 32

HELPING THE FAMILY

Even moving into a new house did not solve all our problems. Our family was always worried about our lack of money. It seemed that we were in debt all the time. The pressure on Baba and Mama brought forth frequent arguments. Sometimes we girls were scolded for minor mistakes. Our family wasn't happy anymore. I worried constantly. We were all under great strain, even Li Hong.

When she turned sixteen on Valentine's Day, 1938, Li Hong dropped out of Lincoln School. She wasn't making any progress in her schoolwork and she preferred working with Mama at home. She was always willing to help.

One day Baba came up with an idea after reading the Want Ads in the newspaper. "Li Hong, you're such a good little housekeeper at home. How would you like to work for a white family as a junior housekeeper? I see an ad in the paper here that a family wants to hire a Chinese girl. Do you want to try it? They will pay you for your work."

"Yes, Baba, I'll do it," Li Hong answered. Li Hong never questioned anything that Baba suggested.

Baba answered the ad and made an appointment for the lady to come to our house to interview Li Hong. When she arrived, Baba spoke to the lady to find out what Li Hong's duties would be and how much she would be paid.

"Li Hong will be our junior housekeeper," the lady said. "We already have a lady housekeeper. Li Hong is to help with dusting, changing the beds, and doing the dishes. She will live with us and have a room by herself. She'll work three hours in the morning, three hours in the afternoon, and one hour after dinner. She will get one day off a week and I'll bring her back here in the morning on her day off. Then I'll come back in the evening to pick her up. Her salary will be twenty-five dollars a month. How does that sound, Mr. Gee?"

Baba and Mama talked this over and agreed to accept the arrangement.

The lady came back the next day to take Li Hong home with her. It wasn't long before the lady reported to Baba, "Li Hong is so sweet and gentle. She follows directions well. We are very pleased with her work."

Baba told us what the lady had said. He seemed very pleased. "I'm so glad that Li Hong is doing well," he said. "Her salary will help our family."

Lai Wah and I yelled, "Hooray for Li Hong!"

Li Hong worked for the family for more than a year. We younger sisters missed her very much. She missed us, too, but she never complained.

One day a Chinese gentleman friend spoke to Baba. This man was an interpreter at Oakland's city hall. He knew that we were struggling to make ends meet. "I know a young man who works for the city," he told Baba. "He needs a junior housekeeper to help his old parents. Do you think Li Keng can do it? He'll come and talk to you about this."

"I'll do it, Baba," I said right away. "I'm twelve years old now. I can do it!" I said.

The gentleman came to our house and interviewed me. His name was Mr. Berger. "My parents are getting older and need someone to help around the house," he said. "There won't be any heavy work. You will work from four to seven every day, Monday through Friday. I'll pay you seventeen dollars a month. Would you like to try it?"

I looked at Baba and said, "I'll do it. You know I want to help earn money for the family. I can drop out of Chinese school. I don't mind."

Mr. Richard Berger shook my hand and said, "Li Keng, you're hired. Can you start next Monday? Take the bus that goes down Foothill Boulevard and get off on Thirty-fourth Avenue. Our house is right there." Mr. Berger shook Baba's hand and my hand and waved good-bye.

That night I thought to myself, I'll be contributing money every month. Maybe Baba and Mama won't worry so much now.

I did drop out of Chinese school. Baba and Mama didn't like it. Neither did I. But my seventeen dollars helped to pay the rent.

I worked for the Berger family for three years and loved it. I thought that the older Mr. and Mrs. Berger were the world's kindest people. They had come to the United States from Germany and had lived in Oakland for many years.

At the Bergers' house I ate German food and learned about German customs. They treated me like a friend and not as a servant. They always invited me to eat dinner with them before I left at seven. Working for this family opened up a brand-new world for me.

Both Li Hong and I felt very proud. Our family was proud of us, too.

Things were finally going more smoothly for us in Gold Mountain. But at the time I had no idea that tragedy would soon threaten our family.

Chapter 33
Dark Days

One day in 1940 the principal of Lincoln School came into my classroom and spoke softly to the teacher. The teacher said, "Li Keng, please go with Mr. Benson."

I looked at her and Mr. Benson in surprise. My teacher gave me a strange, forced smile as Mr. Benson escorted me out of the room.

My heart pounded. Was I in trouble? I couldn't think of anything that I had done wrong.

Lai Wah and a neighbor lady were waiting for me in the office. Mr. Benson said, "Girls, this lady has some news for you."

"You must come home with me right now," our neighbor told us in Chinese. She didn't tell us any news.

"Why?" I asked.

The neighbor replied, "You'll find out when you get home."

I knew something wasn't right. I ran as fast as I could with Lai Wah following me. We rushed into our house and heard Mama sobbing. Two neighbors surrounded her.

"What is wrong, Mama?" I cried. Lai Wah ran to Mama

and threw her arms around her. I just stood there, petrified.

Mama replied, "Your Baba has been shot. He is now at the emergency hospital."

"Baba was shot? Who shot him?" I choked out.

Mama shook her head. "Baba was shot by a man whose last name is also Gee. He was sent to collect money that Baba had borrowed. This man demanded that the loans be paid back in full right away. He threatened Baba with a gun because Baba told him that he didn't have any money. Then the man shot Baba and ran out the door."

Mama began to cry again. "I heard the shots. I dashed into the kitchen and saw Baba on the floor."

Nellie and Leslie were crying now, too. Flo looked terrified.

"I chased the man out on the street," Mama went on. "I yelled for help. I pointed out the man with the gun and two Chinese young men grabbed him. By that time the police arrived and arrested him."

I couldn't say a word. I was too shocked.

Mama kept talking. "Our neighbors called for an ambulance. It was in front of our house when I got home. I couldn't go with Baba to the hospital because my English wasn't good enough for me to tell them what happened. Besides, your sisters needed me at home."

"Oh, Mama, I'm so sorry," I said. "How dare this man do such a thing to Baba?" I sobbed along with Mama. Lai Wah hung on to Mama's sleeves.

"Please, Quan Yin," Mama prayed to the Goddess of Mercy, "take care of my husband."

The telephone rang. It was someone from the hospital. Our neighbor took the call.

"Your Baba is being treated in the intensive care unit by the doctors," the neighbor reported to us. "Right now it's touch and go. We'll have to wait for forty-eight hours to see if your Baba improves. Please, be brave."

Not one of us could eat or sleep that night. It seemed as though our house was covered with a black cloud.

Even though we couldn't stop thinking about Baba, Mama sent Lai Wah and me to school each day. We waited anxiously for the forty-eight hours to pass.

Finally the hospital called and told us that Baba was out of danger. "He'll need to stay here until he is well," they said.

We rejoiced that Baba was going to be okay.

Uncle Jin came from San Francisco to offer his help. Again he gave us money and brought us food. Our kind neighbors brought cooked food for us also. We were grateful for all the support. People were so good to us!

Mama visited Baba at the hospital. Baba's Chinese surgeon spoke to her in Cantonese. "Your husband was shot through his abdomen, left shoulder, and left elbow. His gallbladder, liver, and right kidney were damaged. I had to remove the right kidney. One bullet was aimed at his heart, but it was deflected because your husband had a gold watch in his shirt pocket. The watch saved his life."

Baba told Mama, "I'm going to get out of the lottery business. I'll do something else when I recover fully. No more lottery. The debts can wait."

Baba finally came home after many, many weeks in the hospital. His left arm was in a sling. He gave us a big smile as he walked through the door. Mama and all of us sisters beamed with joy.

"Baba, welcome home!" we girls all yelled.

But I still worried, even when Baba was on the mend at home. What was going to happen next? Would our money troubles ever be over for good?

Chapter 34
A New Life

Baba wasn't able to work for more than a year. His insurance paid him fifty dollars a month for his disability. Li Hong and I continued to contribute our salaries. That was all the money our family had.

Our neighbors knew that we were still very poor. One of them suggested that we apply for welfare. That made Mama very upset. "What?" she said. "The Gees won't do that. Even though we are poor, taking money from the government is shameful. Thank you for your suggestion. But we'll manage somehow."

Mama took charge of the family now because Baba wasn't able to. She went to a shrimp wholesale place to ask if we could shell shrimp for them.

When she got home Mama told us older girls firmly, "No more playing hopscotch or jumping rope. You must use every minute outside of school or work to pitch in and help make money."

Every Saturday Mama, Lai Hong, Lai Wah, and I sat around the kitchen table, carefully shelling the small shrimp. After the job was finished, Mama returned the shelled shrimp, packed in ice, to the wholesaler. On a good day, we were able to earn about five dollars. The money took care of our grocery bill for the week.

Baba couldn't help us in the kitchen because his left arm was still in a sling. However, he looked at the want ads in the newspaper for job opportunities. He saw a small grocery store for sale in Berkeley. "Do you think we can try our hand at running a grocery store?" he asked Mama. "I'll call the owners. If the price is right, may I go ahead and sign the papers to buy the store? Well, what do you think, Mama?"

"Yes, go ahead," Mama answered. She sounded very tired. "Maybe we could make a living this way. Anything is better than a lottery business."

Baba bought the little grocery store with money that he borrowed from relatives. The store came with a kitchen in the back. It had a refrigerator, a stove, a table, and some chairs.

An idea clicked in Baba's head when he saw the kitchen. "Why don't we sell *chow mein* along with groceries? You're a good cook, Mama. You can cook the *chow mein* noodles. I'll put a sign in the window. We'll see if people are interested."

The idea pleased Mama.

The big sign said, "Pork Chow Mein to Go! 50 cents an order. Freshly Cooked Here!"

It turned out many people wanted to buy Mama's home-cooked food.

Each morning Baba and Mama stocked the refrigerator with all the ingredients for the *chow mein*. We bought *char sui*, Chinese roast pork, from Chinatown. When customers placed their orders, Mama went back to the kitchen and cooked the pork with noodles in a wok. A wok is a round frying pan with a rounded bottom that sits on top of a circular piece of metal so it won't tilt.

Mama boxed each order of *chow mein* in a take-out carton. Customers returned again and again. They told Baba and Mama that the *chow mein* was delicious. Baba was pleased for coming up with the idea.

Although the grocery store business made a small profit, we still needed more money to pay back all that we had borrowed from our relatives. But this time I knew we could do it.

Chapter 35

GOOD LUCK AT LAST

Baba and Mama enjoyed working at the grocery store. They were happy that our family no longer had anything to do with the lottery business. They didn't scold us as much. Their happiness rubbed off on us girls.

About a year later, Baba decided to sell the grocery store. Mama was pregnant again. It was getting very hard for her to go to Berkeley and work at the store.

We all noticed Mama's stomach was much larger this time. She waddled slowly and her face had a special glow. She said, "I know it'll be a boy this time!" The rest of us believed it, too.

Summer came and on the morning of July 7, 1941, Mama said, "Call Dr. Lam and Mrs. Young. The baby is coming!"

Baba quickly telephoned Dr. Lam and Mrs. Young. They arrived almost immediately. All of us were very excited.

I hope it's a boy, I hope it's a boy, I told myself over and over.

Lai Wah kept the younger girls busy by playing with them in another part of the house. Li Hong and I stayed near Mama's room just in case we were needed. "Don't make too much noise, little sisters!" I ordered.

We could hear Mama moaning. We knew she was in pain.

Finally we heard Baba yell, "It's a boy! It's a boy!" He sounded overjoyed.

Li Hong and I heard the baby cry as Dr. Lam and Mrs. Young cleaned him up. Then Dr. Lam weighed the baby with a handheld scale. He weighed over ten pounds and the scale broke. Baba grabbed the baby and held on. It was a scary moment.

Dr. Lam finished taking care of Mama. She asked, "Mr. Gee, do you want me to give an American name to your son?"

Baba smiled and shook his head. "Thank you, Dr. Lam, but we already have a name for this baby. We'll call him William, because it is a name of kings and heroes."

Dr. Lam smiled, "Yes, it's a name that fits this baby. Congratulations, Mr. and Mrs. Gee. I'm happy for all of you."

After Dr. Lam left, Mama slept for a long time. When she woke up, Baba announced, "I'm going to give William a Chinese name now, Mama. We'll call him Wah Kung, which means 'strong China.' Do you like it?"

"Yes, William and Wah Kung are beautiful names," Mama answered with a smile. "Oh, Baba, at last we have a son to carry on our family name. Quan Yin, Goddess of Mercy, answered our prayers. From this day on, I know our lives will get better. We will be so happy!"

Baba quickly telephoned friends and relatives about our new baby brother. In no time at all everyone in Chinatown heard the good news and rejoiced with us. Little William became quite a celebrity.

After a month, William had a grand Red Egg party. Friends, relatives, and neighbors were invited to the celebration. He received a great number of packages of *lay see*. Baba opened a bank account for him for his future college education. William was the only one of us to have a bank account.

William was a handsome baby with a full head of dark hair. His chubby cheeks begged to be touched. All of us older sisters doted on him. Baba and Mama adored him, too. William brought lots of happiness. Our family was complete.

Chapter 36

A VERY SPECIAL YEAR

At last we had a boy to carry on our family name. It seemed as though brother William brought sparkling sunbeams into our house. Everyone in the family smiled all the time.

The other good news was that the doctor finally gave Baba permission to go back to work.

Baba knew that the shipyards needed workers to build ships. Baba and Li Hong found jobs as welders. Welding paid better than other jobs. Baba taught Li Hong how to use the welding torch. They worked the night shift because night shift workers were paid more.

Every evening I watched Li Hong tie her hair under a bandana. Then she put her hard hat on top of her head. She wore safety goggles and thick leather gloves. Baba did, too.

Baba had Li Hong work next to him to make sure that she was all right. The two of them came home in the early morning. It was hard work but their paychecks helped Baba pay back some of the money we owed.

"Li Hong, do you like working as a welder?" I asked my sister. "Are there other women working on the ship?"

She nodded. "Yes, to both questions. It is a good job."

I was very proud of my sister. Everyone else in the family was, too.

In June of 1941, I graduated from the ninth grade. I sewed my own pretty cotton dress for the graduation ceremony. I left Lincoln School with many happy memories.

After graduation I told the Bergers that I couldn't continue to work for them anymore. I needed time to study my high school subjects. The Bergers were sad but they understood.

"Thank you for allowing me to work for you the past three years," I said. "You've been very kind. I'll never forget you." Tears streamed down my face as I hugged them both.

"Good-bye, Li Keng. Enjoy your life in the United States. You've been an excellent helper. We'll always remember you, too!" Mr. Berger told me.

Mr. and Mrs. Berger and their son walked me to the bus stop and waved good-bye until I boarded the bus. I waved back until the bus turned the corner.

Our family had lived in Gold Mountain for seven years. We loved living in our new country, even though we were still poor. We knew it was better than living back in Goon Do Hung, our old village in China. We were all getting to be more like Americans now.

On December 2, 1941, Baba looked at the calendar. He called, "Mama and girls, please gather around. I have good news to tell you. You four ladies from China are now citizens of the United States. People who immigrate from another country must live here for seven years before they can become citizens. You don't have to take citizenship tests. You don't have to be sworn in. I am very happy and I know you are, too."

We all celebrated this wonderful news.

I said, "Baba, please write a letter to Cousin Soe in Goon Do Hung. She'll love to hear from us. Tell her that we are in good health. Tell her that Gold Mountain, the United States, is a great country. Tell her that you have six daughters and one son. Baby William has brought much happiness to our family. Tell her that someday I would like to return to Goon Do Hung for a visit. Wish Cousin Soe good health."

Baba answered, "All right, Li Keng. I'll write the letter today."

At last my dream had come true. I was an American now. I loved living in Gold Mountain. Our long journey had been a miracle for me and for my family.

Author's Note

After Mama, Li Hong, Lai Wah, and I became American citizens, our lives continued to improve.

Baba and Mama opened a Chinese and American restaurant in Oakland's Chinatown in 1943. Business was good from the first day. Shipyard workers, families, and other people came to eat our good food. Baba and Mama worked eighteen hours a day, seven days a week. After three months, Baba paid back all the money he owed our relatives.

We three older girls waited tables. Li Hong worked most days because she was no longer attending school. Mama couldn't afford a baby-sitter for Bill, so he went to the restaurant with her every day. He sat happily in a corner, coloring pictures and playing quietly.

Our family sold the restaurant when Baba died in 1961. Mama stayed at home until she moved to a retirement home near Chinatown. She died in 1973.

Li Hong raised three children. She is now eighty-three years old and lives in San Francisco with Henry, her husband. They have two adult grandsons.

Lai Wah was a stay-at-home mom for some years after her two daughters were born. She has three grandchildren. She

Gee family portrait in 1944, the year I graduated from high school: (left to right) Nellie, me, Mama, Li Hong, Bill, Henry Lew (Li Hong's husband), Baba, Lai Wah, Flo, and Leslie

now volunteers at a senior center and was recognized as an Outstanding Volunteer of the Year.

Nellie is the author of three collections of poetry. Two of her poems are inscribed in concrete at public sites in San Francisco. She retired after working in the business world for forty-six years.

Leslie worked for the Oakland Schools as an administrative assistant. She died in 1985, leaving behind three children.

Flo taught school for a number of years. She attended UC Berkeley and Cal State Hayward. She has two children and one grandson. Today she is a mixed media installation artist. Her work has been exhibited on Angel Island and Ellis Island in New York. Among her many awards, she received the 1995 President's Award from the Women's Caucus for Art.

William is a well-known journalist. He has one son. Bill attended UC Berkeley and received his master's degree from Columbia University. He worked for the *Wall Street Journal* and *Oakland Tribune* and taught journalism and Asian-American Studies. He received numerous awards in his field. Today he is a freelance writer with two published books, *Yellow Journalist* and *Oakland's Chinatown*.

I achieved my dream of becoming a teacher of young children. I taught elementary school for thirty-five years after graduating from UC Berkeley. I have a son and a daughter. My three grandchildren bring me lots of happiness.

After I retired from teaching, I was asked by Walt Disney Studios to take part in the filming of a documentary called *The American Tapestry*. The film tells several immigrants' stories, including ours. I often use the video when I give lectures

Baba and Mama with Bill in their restaurant. The baby is Victoria Lew, Li Hong's first child.

*Left to right: Flo, Nellie, Melvin Lew (Li Hong's son),
Leslie, Bill, and Victoria Lew*

to people about my Angel Island experience. The film shows
my return with some family members to our old village in
China. It is much the same today as it was when I was a child.

Our whole family still lives in the greater San Francisco Bay
Area. We touch base often and remain very close. Li Hong,
Lai Wah, and I will never forget our journey to Gold
Mountain and the joys and opportunities our new country has
given us.

GOOD FORTUNE

MORE ABOUT ANGEL ISLAND IMMIGRATION STATION AND THE CHINESE EXCLUSION ACT

When news of the California Gold Rush reached China in the 1800s, the United States gained the Chinese nickname "Gum Saan," or "Gold Mountain." Many Chinese workers, especially those barely scraping out a living in China's rural provinces, made great sacrifices to leave China and start new lives in this land of opportunity.

However, the reality of America was anything but a fairy tale for many of these Chinese immigrants. One of their greatest challenges was fitting into a society that viewed them as cheap laborers who stole jobs from white Americans. The first immigration law to restrict a particular race, the Chinese Exclusion Act of 1882, turned this prejudice into law, severely restricting the number of Chinese people who could enter the United States. All Chinese workers were now excluded from coming to the United States, with the exception of a few elite classes such as diplomats and students. Family members of Chinese people already in the country were also allowed.

Early Chinese immigrants, mostly men, came to Gum Saan to find work. Many of them left a wife and children back in their villages, and they sent money they earned in the U.S. back to their families in China. The husbands and families were often separated for many years.

Many Chinese immigrants traveled back to China. When some of these men returned to the United States, they falsely reported to the immigration people that a son had been born to them. (They seldom reported that a daughter had been born. Even if they had had a daughter, they might still claim

Angel Island

that a son had been born.) Later, they would sell the papers to a male friend or relative so they could bring someone from China to the United States. That is where the term "paper son" comes from.

A number of Chinese people soon became "paper sons" or "paper daughters" of Chinese-Americans, meaning that they pretended to have family relationships to circumvent the laws.

Aware of this deception, the response from the U.S. government was not at all sympathetic. In 1910 the U.S. government opened the Angel Island Immigration Station on a small island in San Francisco Bay. The facility was intended to provide a more secure processing and holding area for immigrants who crossed the Pacific Ocean. While immigrants from Russia, Australia, Japan, Korea, and other countries also passed through the station gates, the great bulk of detainees were Chinese.

Li Keng Gee and her family were among the 175,000 Chinese immigrants who came to America through Angel Island during its operation from 1910 to 1940. The facility had separate barracks for men and women that were kept under guard at all times. Immigrants were first given probing medical exams, which were especially humiliating to the modest Chinese. Most unsettling were the long interrogations by the Bureau of Immigration Services about their personal lives and their reasons for coming to the U.S. The questioning might last weeks or months or even years.

The conditions that led to the restriction of Chinese immigration slowly began to ease during the early 1900s. Because fewer Chinese immigrants were entering the U.S., the Chinese were no longer seen as a threat. Other immigrants—such as the Japanese—began to bear the brunt of American suspicion. The Angel Island Immigration Station closed following a fire in 1940 and never reopened. The Chinese Exclusion Act was finally repealed in 1943, soon after China became an American ally in World War II. Chinese immigration remained severely restricted until 1965.

For Further Information

Web Resources:

Angel Island Immigration Station Foundation—
www.aiisf.org
Angel Island State Park—*www.angelisland.org*
Lum, Lydia. "Angel Island: Journeys Remembered by
Chinese Houstonians: An Oral History of Chinese
Immigrant Detainees"—*www.chron.com/content/
chronicle/special/angelisland/index.html*
Library of Congress, American Memory historical collection:
"Chinese Immigration"—*www.memory.loc.gov/learn/
features/immig/chinese.html*

Other Resources for Young Readers:

ANGEL ISLAND IMMIGRANT JOURNEYS: A CURRICULUM GUIDE,
available from *www.aiisf.org.*
Currier, Katrina Saltonstall. KAI'S JOURNEY TO GOLD
MOUNTAIN. Tiburon: Angel Island Association, 2004.
Hoobler, Dorothy and Thomas. THE CHINESE AMERICAN
FAMILY ALBUM. London: Oxford University Press, 1994.
Takaki, Ronald. JOURNEY TO GOLD MOUNTAIN: THE CHINESE
IN 19TH CENTURY AMERICA. New York: Chelsea House
Publishers, 1994.

About the Author

THE FIRST PERSON in her family to attend college, Li Keng Wong taught elementary school in the San Francisco Bay area for more than thirty-five years. Now retired, she often shares her family's immigration experiences with schools and community organizations. An avid supporter of the Angel Island Immigration Station, Ms. Wong enjoys reading, volunteering at local senior centers, playing mah jong, and spending time with her three grandchildren. She lives in a small city across the bay from San Francisco. GOOD FORTUNE is her first book for young readers.